THE STORY OF THE
PADDLE STEAMER

TO MY FATHER

Who first introduced me to a
paddle steamer.

THE STORY OF THE
PADDLE
STEAMER

BY

BERNARD DUMPLETON

MELKSHAM
COLIN VENTON

ISBN 0 85475 057 6

Printed in Great Britain at the Press of the Publisher The Uffington Press, Melksham, Wiltshire, SN12 6LA, (U.K.)

LIST OF CONTENTS

LIST OF ILLUSTRATIONS

Jacket Illustration—The *Crested Eagle* passing Chapmans Light on the Thames. From the painting by J. Spurling (Courtesy General Steam Navigation Co.)

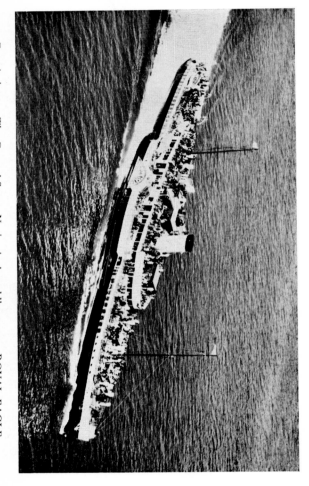

Frontispiece — The General Steam Navigation's paddle steamer ROYAL EAGLE. (Photo courtesy of Southern Ferries).

INTRODUCTION

FROM the very beginning of the Industrial Revolution steam power has been successfully applied to all forms of transport except aircraft, and even that has been tried. Nowhere, however, has the application been more successful than in marine engineering. Whether it be in the form of reciprocating or turbine engines steam has been the driving force for the majority of the world's ships for over 100 years. In the development of marine engineering the paddle steamer held a unique place. The first faltering steps with simple 'atmospheric' engines were taken using the paddle-wheel as the driving medium. Steam engines developed rapidly and before long the paddle steamer moved from the rivers and canals onto the oceans.

Their life there was short once the superiority of the screw had been proved, but the advantages of shallow draft and good manoeuvrability were still important on the inland and coastal waters. All over the world the paddle steamers became a familiar sight on rivers and lakes and around the coastlines. They provided essential links with remote places and connected the big cities to the sea.

Then came the railways.

Faster and more direct they crossed rivers and traversed the land in an intricate network which ensured that there were few places which could not be reached quickly and in comfort. The paddle steamers fell back on pleasure excursion work, and for a while this was their major role, but the coming of the motor-coach and private car gave the public greater independence.

Two World Wars, in which the paddlers served gallantly, bit savagely into their ranks. Operating costs mounted and owners were forced to sell off their fleets. In the years after the Second World War they did so with such rapidity that the paddle steamers became almost extinct. Only the efforts of a few people who recognised the historical importance of these vessels ensured that they did not completely disappear.

The story of the paddle steamer covers approximately 150 years. This book tells that story from its beginning to the present day. It tells of the men who built and designed them, who made and lost fortunes, who saw their dreams realised or shattered. It also tells of the men who sailed in them, often with only their experience under sail to draw upon, men who could barely read or write, but had the mariner's instinct for knowing the sea and respecting its authority.

But above all it tells the story of the paddle steamers, their triumphs and tragedies, their rise and decline on the oceans of the world and on the waterways of Britain, America and Australia.

Technical details have been kept to a minimum and are given only where they are important or are of special interest. There are many vessels which have not been mentioned, to list every paddle steamer ever built would be an impossible task, but in writing this book it has been my aim to show the part that these wonderful vessels have played in maritime history. Older readers will, I hope, be reminded of pre-war days when a paddle steamer trip was a memorable event. The younger generation, brought up on hovercraft and jet-power, will perhaps feel that there is something they have missed, and will be encouraged to seek out the few remaining paddlers and join forces with those who wish to see them preserved.

Bernard Dumpleton
St. Albans. 1973

Chapter One

THE PIONEERS

THE paddle-wheel has been in use for centuries. There is
evidence that the Romans experimented with paddle-
wheels in ships, using oxen to supply the power. It would
seem that the experiments were not very successful as the
long-oared galley is best known as the typical vessel of
those times. The Chinese are believed to have used
man-powered paddle-wheels in their warships during the
seventh century and throughout the ages various ideas
have been put forward to use this form of propulsion.

Leonardo da Vinci, who invented just about everything,
produced drawings in the year 1500 showing a vessel
paddle-propelled and driven by two pedals, thus anticipat-
ing the 'pedalo' by some four centuries. In 1543 a Spanish
sea-captain, Blasco de Garay, submitted plans to the
Emperor Carlos V for a machine that would propel a ship
'without the aid of oars or sail'. The idea is said to have
been tried in a ship called Trinidad in Barcelona Bay. The
paddle-wheels were each turned by 25 men and the vessel
attained a speed of 3.5 m.p.h.

The development of steam power also has a long history,
starting with Hero of Alexandria's re-action device in
about A.D. 50.

11

Many scientists and inventors of the past wrote vaguely about the possibility of 'driving up water by fire', but it was Denis Papin, a Frenchman, who first proposed the use of steam to propel a ship. It is known that he built a paddle boat in 1707, but whether it was driven by steam or 'par la force humaine' is a subject of argument among historians. The following year Papin submitted a paper to the Royal Society proposing the construction of a steam-boat. The proposal was never acted upon, but it would appear that Papin was the first man to see the possibility of a practical paddle steamer.

After Papin's death, in 1714, numerous attempts to harness steam-power for ship propulsion were made, particularly in France.

In 1783 the Marquis De Jouffroy D'Abbans launched his steamboat, the 'Pyroscaphe', on the river Saone, near Lyons. It sailed under steam power for 15 minutes. The engine was a horizontal, double acting cylinder of 25.6 inches diameter with a stroke of 77 inches. The piston rod operated a double ratchet mechanism which produced a continuous rotative motion at the paddle-shaft.

Many of the engines used in these early experiments were designed by, or based on the design of, the English steam pioneer Thomas Newcomen. Newcomen himself had little interest in marine engineering and it was left to William Symington to design an engine for steamboat experiments.

In 1788 Symington was commissioned by Patrick Miller, a wealthy banker, who had earlier experimented with manual paddle-ships. The engine, which is still preserved in the Science Museum in London, consisted of two vertical cylinders, 4 inches diameter by 18 inches stroke. The two pistons were connected by chains to a drum which rotated in opposite directions alternately. The two paddle-wheels were mounted on shafts on each of which were two pulleys with internal ratchet teeth. Between each pair of pulleys was a disc fitted with two pawls. The pulleys were turned in opposite directions by chains from the drum and the teeth on the ratchet wheels engaged with the pawls to drive the paddle-wheels continuously in one direction.

The boat was double-hulled, catarmaran style, and the engine was located in one hull with the boiler in the other. The paddle-wheels were placed between the hulls in tandem. Principal dimensions of the boat were: displacement, about five tons, length 25ft, breadth 7ft, and draught 2.2ft. On October 14th, 1788, the vessel was tried on Dalwinston Lake, near Dumfries, and reached a speed of 5 m.p.h. On board were Miller, Symington, James Taylor, Alexander Nasmyth and the poet, Robert Burns.

Two years earlier, the American inventor, John Fitch, had achieved some success with an extraordinary contrivance which used 12 vertical oars. The oars were mounted six on each side and were operated by a steam engine of Fitch's own design.

As the six forward oars dipped and rose from the water they were followed by the rear bank of six and so propelled the ship in canoe-like fashion. Fitch followed this with a larger version in 1788, and two days before Patrick Miller's experiment the vessel steamed from Philadelphia to Burlington on the Delaware river, a distance of 20 miles. There were thirty passengers on board and the average speed for the journey was 5.5 knots.

After the success of his engine in the Miller boat, Symington obtained financial aid from Lord Dundas of Kerse, and in 1801 was launched the vessel that is reckoned to be the first successful steamship.

The *Charlotte Dundas* was built of wood by Alexander Hart at Grangemouth, Stirlingshire, and was 56ft long with a beam of 18ft and a depth of 8ft. Symington introduced several improvements in the design of the engine, a single, direct acting cylinder was used, 22 inches diameter and 4ft stroke. The engine developed 10 nominal horse-power (N.H.P.) and drove a single, rear-mounted paddle via an overhanging crank on the paddle-shaft. The paddle-wheel was housed in a recess 4ft wide by 12ft long and was totally enclosed. It was the intention of Lord Dundas to use the vessel on the Forth and Clyde Canal as a steam tug. In March 1802 trials were carried out and the *Charlotte Dundas* hauled two 70-ton barges over a distance of 19.5 miles in six hours, and this against a strong headwind.

The canal owners, however, were not impressed. They claimed that the wash from the vessel would damage the canal bank and banned its use. Symington was reduced to poverty and died in 1831. The *Charlotte Dundas* was left abandoned in a creek and was broken up in 1861.

The shortsightedness of the canal owners robbed Britain of being the home of the first commercially successful steamboat. That honour must go to the American, Robert Fulton and his ship the P.S. *Clermont*. Fulton had visited Scotland and gained much useful knowledge from his observations of the *Charlotte Dundas* trials. He worked in France for a time and his first steamboat ran trials on the River Seine, but it was on the Hudson River in New York that the *Clermont* achieved success.

The vessel was 133ft in length with a breadth of 13ft and a draught of 2ft. Displacement was 100 tons. The engine was British, supplied by Messrs. Boulton, Watt & Co. and was of 20 nominal h.p. The single cylinder, 24 inches diameter by 4ft stroke, drove two side paddle-wheels of 15ft diameter through a series of bellcranks and spur gears designed by Fulton. The first trial took place on 17th August, 1807, and the speed attained was 4.7 m.p.h.

The *Clermont* ran as a packet between New York and Albany until 1807-8 when she was rebuilt and renamed *North River*. She then continued to serve for another seven years.

Fulton was not only a clever engineer but a good businessman as well. He gained the monopoly of the steamboat trade on the Hudson and was thereby indirectly responsible for the first sea-going voyage of a paddle-steamer. Two other Americans, John Stevens and his son Robert, built their paddle steamer *Phoenix* in 1807 at Hoboken, New York. But because of Fulton's monopoly they were forced to take the ship via the open sea to Philadelphia where she ran as a packet for several years. The voyage was made in a severe gale and is, therefore, all the more remarkable for a vessel built for river work.

Britain, and Europe, had to wait until 1812 before a paddle steamer was built that was to run a regular service.

Henry Bell's *Comet,* begun in 1811, was named after the comet of that year. Her hull had bluff lines with a clipper stem and square stern. Principle dimensions were: length 51ft, breadth over paddle-boxes 15ft and draught 4ft. *Comet*'s engines were built by John Robertson of Glasgow and is now preserved in the Science Museum in London. It had a vertical cylinder, 12.5 inches diameter by 16 inches stroke, and drove two rods and half side levers via a crosshead. A connecting rod worked the overhanging crankshaft which carried a 6ft flywheel and a spur gear for driving the paddle-wheels. The *Comet* had a tall funnel to which was attached a yardarm and sail, a feature which was to be copied in many subsequent steamships.

The ship was not an instant success. Clydesiders viewed her with suspicion, maintaining that it was only a matter of time before she blew up. Such gloomy predictions brought scores of children to the river bank every time she passed by, but they were to be disappointed. Soon the *Comet* was a familiar sight on the river, gradually the fears were overcome and the ship became an object of affection. In 1819 Bell used the vessel between the West Highlands and Glasgow. The following year she ran ashore at Craignish Point and was totally wrecked.

The success of the *Comet* encouraged other boat builders and in 1814 another paddle steamer, the *Margery,* appeared on the Clyde. The *Margery* was slightly larger than the *Comet,* 73ft overall with a 10 n.p.h. engine, and she also used her tall single funnel as a mainmast.

After running on the Clyde for a short time she was purchased by Messrs. Anthony Cortis and Co., of London, but transporting her to the Thames presented something of a problem. She was too wide to pass through the locks on the Forth and Clyde canal so her paddle-wheels and sponsons were removed to allow her to be towed up to the Firth of Forth. From there she sailed down the east coast, using her mainsail and entered the Thames in January 1815. Only a few days after her arrival she was at work, operating a public service between London and Gravesend on alternate days. At the end of her first season the steamer was sold to a French firm and renamed *Elise.* Under the command of her new captain she sailed to Newhaven and thence across the Channel to Havre.

This was the first Channel crossing by a steamship, a journey that took seventeen hours in strong southerly winds.

The *Margery*'s appearance on the Thames was greeted with astonishment by Londoners, for to many of them she was something entirely new. History books generally acknowledge her as being the first paddle steamer to operate on the Thames, but in the previous year a small steamer had gone into service on the London-Richmond route. She was the *Richmond,* a 50-ton vessel with a 10 h.p. Maudslay bell-crank engine. Like the *Comet* she was greeted with considerable apprehension. The Watermen, who saw their trade jeopardised by the new vessel, fostered the fears with stories of fire and boiler explosions.

Unfortunately their predictions came true, for on the

28th June, 1817, her boiler burst just after the steamer had passed under Westminster Bridge on her way to Richmond.

Despite this and various other mishaps the popularity of the paddle steamers grew. The country's shipyards began to build them in growing numbers and regular services were established from London to Gravesend, Greenock to Belfast and Holyhead to Dublin. In 1821 the 90 ton steamer *Rob Roy* started the Dover-Calais service.

These short sea crossings disproved the belief that paddle steamers, or 'butterfly boats' as the deep sea sailors called them, were too frail for sea-going voyages .

Their ruggedness was further proved by the remarkable voyage of the P.S. *Thames*. Originally named *Argyle,* the steamer was built at Glasgow in 1814 and worked on the Clyde for a while. In 1815 she was sold to a London company who were faced with the same trouble of delivery as that encountered by the owners of the *Margery*. Rather than make the structural alterations necessary to move her through the Forth and Clyde canal it was decided to take the ship down the west coast via Milford Haven and Lands End.

The steamer left Glasgow in May 1815 with a crew of nine and crossed first to Dublin. Heavy seas kept her speed down to 3 knots and her 16 h.p. engines and 9ft diameter paddle-wheels must have been hard put to maintain headway.

On 28th May she sailed for Wexford and thence to Milford Haven. During this part of the journey there was trouble with the paddle-wheels and one floatboard had to be cut from each. Continuing around Lands End she was twice approached by boats from the shore where onlookers had reported that she was on fire. She was, in fact, the first steamer to be seen in those waters. The voyage continued without further incident up the Channel and on to the Thames where she reached London on 12th

June. A month later the ship went into service on the London-Margate run, and a report in the Times of 8th July 1815 described her as a rapid, spacious and splendid vessel with well appointed cabins, a choice library and a stewardess to attend upon the needs of the fair sex.

The P.S. *Thames* ran on this route for one season after which she was withdrawn in favour of a larger vessel, the *Regent*. The *Regent*'s career was also shortlived, but she was a ship worthy of mention as she was the first steamboat to be built on the river Thames. Her engines drove each paddle-wheel independently and she was lightly constructed to obtain high speed. On July 2nd, 1817, the ship caught fire whilst off Whitstable and was completely burnt out. The 40 passengers and crew of 10 were all rescued by boats putting off from the shore.

Fire was an ever-present hazard on these early vessels built, as they were, entirely of wood.

Their furnaces were often of the external type and the danger from red-hot ashes and sparks led to a number of ships being completely destroyed. The danger was lessened in the iron-built ships that followed, and the first to be built was the *Aaron Manby*. The ship was laid down at the Horseley Iron Works near Tipton, Staffordshire, in 1821. The master of the works was Aaron Manby and the new vessel was a joint venture between Manby, his son Charles and Captain Charles Napier, later Admiral Sir Charles Napier. The hull was constructed of quarter-inch thick iron plates lapped and riveted. The single deck was of wood, as were the beams that supported it.

The vessel was designed for cargo-carrying and the hold was separated from the engine room by two bulkheads, one of iron and the other of wood.

The 47ft tall funnel ensured that sparks would be carried well away from the deck and, as was the practice of the day, it also served as a mast. The engines, rated at 30 n.p.h., consisted of two oscillating cylinders and were designed by Aaron Manby. Two 12ft diameter paddle-wheels, with floats 30 inches wide, were fitted and the ship had an average speed of 7 knots. This was quite a respectable speed for a ship of her size; 120ft long, 23ft wide and a burden of 116 tons.

The hull was transported in sections from the Horseley works to Rotherhithe on the Thames where the final assembly was completed.

Trials took place in May 1822 and the first commercial voyage was made the following month. Under the command of Captain Napier, and with Charles Manby as engineer, the *Aaron Manby* crossed the Channel to Havre with a cargo of iron and linseed. From there she proceeded up the River Seine to Paris, where the sight of an iron ship caused great surprise and considerable disbelief. But another step forward in the development of the steamship had been taken. The *Aaron Manby* was the first iron-built vessel to put to sea, and the first ship to sail direct from London to Paris.

And so the steamship was born. During the thirty years after Patrick Miller's first success the development of the paddle steamer made rapid progress.

Their shallow draught and the good manoeuvrability made them particularly suitable for river and coastal work, and it was in those waters that they were to reign supreme for 150 years. Before long the marine engineers of the time began to consider the possibilities of the paddle steamer as an ocean-going vessel. Opposition from the ship-owners was strong. This was the era of the wind-jammers and clipper ships, ships that could travel at speeds that would be no disgrace today, if the wind and tide was in their favour. But the advantages of travelling in a straight line, regardless of the elements, could not be ignored. In 1818 an American schooner, the *Savannah,* was fitted with an auxiliary engine and paddles.

On 24th May, 1819, she left Savannah, bound for

Liverpool. The voyage attracted a great deal of attention and the *Savannah* is often described as the first steamship to cross the Atlantic. In fact her engines were used only for about 80 hours of the journey, but it marked the beginning of the steamship on the oceans of the world.

Fig. 1 — CHARLOTTE DUNDAS. Pioneer steamboat of 1802.
(Photo Science Museum, London).

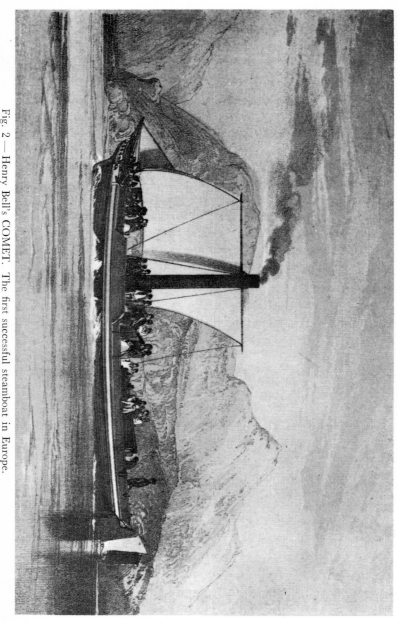

Fig. 2 — Henry Bell's COMET. The first successful steamboat in Europe. (Photo Science Museum, London).

Chapter Two

OCEAN PADDLE STEAMERS

The Atlantic highway — P.S. *Savannah* — *Sirius* v *Great Western* — The birth of the Cunard Company — Competition with the Collins' Line — Pacific and Orient.

THE era of the ocean-going paddle steamer started with the voyage of the *Savannah* in 1819, and ended when the P.S. *Scotia* was withdrawn from service in 1875. It was a transitional period during which the paddle steamer served as a link between the sailing ships and the screw-driven ocean liners. Once the superiority of the screw had been demonstrated, by Brunel's S.S. *Great Britain* in 1843, it was only a matter of time before the paddlers disappeared from the world's oceans. But it was a period which set the pattern for the great steamship lines that became world famous names. The first regular trans-Atlantic service, the Blue Riband competition and the birth of such companies as Cunard and P & O all occurred within those fifty-six years.

The P.S. *Savannah* was built as a schooner for the packet service from New York to Havre in France. Before her completion she was bought by the Savannah Steam Ship Company and was fitted with an auxiliary steam-engine and collapsible paddle-wheels. The engine consisted of a single cylinder, 40 inches diameter by 5ft stroke, which operated on extremely low pressure; less than 1 pound per square inch. The design of the paddle-wheels was unique. Each had ten radial arms linked together by chains and could be folded like a fan. The whole assembly could then be taken on board and stowed away, an operation that took about twenty minutes. When under steam power alone the ship had a speed of about 4 knots. The new owners had intended to use her on coastal services but a trade depression forced them to offer the ship for sale and Europe was chosen as a likely market. On May 24th, 1819, she left her home port bound for Liverpool under the command of Captain Moses Rogers who had captained the *Phoenix* on her sea-going voyage (see Chapter One).

No passengers were carried and the fuel on board amounted to 75 tons of coal and 25 cords of wood.

The sails were used for most of the voyage but apparently her engine was used for the latter part of the journey for when she was sighted off the coast of Ireland she was reported as being a ship on fire. Consumption of coal had been heavy and the ship refuelled at Kinsale before steaming to Liverpool where she arrived on the 20th of June. The voyage had taken 27 days and 11 hours. The paddle-wheels were used only once when the wind was insufficient to provide a speed of more than 4 knots. As a sales trip the voyage was a disaster. After being offered in various countries, including Russia where it was hoped to interest Tsar Alexander I, the *Savannah* returned to America and was finally sold by auction. Her engine was removed and she worked as a sail packet until being wrecked on Long Island in 1821.

As the *Savannah*'s return trip was made entirely under sail, the first east-west Atlantic crossing by a steamship was made by the first British steam warship, the P.S. *Rising Star*.

Although ordered in 1818 she was not laid down until 1820 and ran her trials in June 1821 on the Thames. The vessel had three keels with two paddle-wheels set either side of the centre keel. The engines were 70 n.h.p., twin cylinder, constructed by Maudslay Sons and Field. She was a full-rigged ship, with three masts, two funnels and ten gunports on each side. The warship had been intended for use in the Chilean revolution and she sailed from Gravesend for Valparaiso on 22nd October, 1821. After springing a leak and putting into Cork for repairs she eventually arrived at her destination on April 22nd, 1822, by which time the revolution was over. The extent to which steampower was used is not known, but she is said to have reached a speed of 12 knots.

The difficulties of making an Atlantic crossing under continuous steam power were caused, not so much by the unreliability of the engines but by the fact that coal consumption was high and the boilers used sea-water. Consequently the engines were used sparingly and the boilers had to be cleaned regularly. In 1827 a Dutch steamer, the 438-ton *Curacao,* sailed 4,000 miles from Holland to South America in 28 days using steam power for much of the way. Although Dutch owned she was British built by J. H. and J. Duke at Dover in 1825. Originally named *Calpe* she was sold to the Dutch in 1826. During the long voyage the engines were stopped several times for routine boiler cleaning and repairs to the paddle-wheels. One problem was that as coal was consumed, at the rate of 5 tons a day, so the ship rose in the water thereby impairing the efficiency of the paddles. The original paddle-wheel diameter of 15ft was extended to 16ft and later to 17ft to allow for this unforeseen difficulty. On her second crossing in 1828, the engines were used continuously for 13 days and the time was reduced to 25 days.

One uneventful, and therefore notable, west to east crossing was made in 1831 by the Canadian built *Royal William*. The ship was partly owned by Samuel Cunard who later founded the Cunard Line. Few details are known about the ship except that the paddle-wheels were built inside the hull, but the 28-days' voyage was made almost entirely under steam, the boilers being de-salted every fourth day.

All these voyages represented the first tottering steps towards the advent of the true ocean-going liner. The year 1838 may be described as a vintage year for the ocean paddle steamers, for it marked the real beginning of regular passenger services and the introduction of steam-ships specifically designed for the trade.

In that year three British concerns opened up regular steamship services to New York. They were the Great Western Steamship Company, the British and American Steam Navigation Company and the Trans-Atlantic Steamship Company.

Rivalry between the three was keen, and the bid to be first with a ship that would cross using entirely steam power led to an exciting climax when all three achieved success within the space of four months. Ironically the pride of place for the first-ever all-steam crossing of the Atlantic goes to a ship that was not designed for ocean steaming. The P.S. *Sirius* was a cross-channel steamer belonging to the St. George Steam Packet Company. Built in 1837 she had a displacement of 700 tons, and was 178ft long with a breadth of 26ft. She was, in fact, too large for her trade but still hardly suitable for the North Atlantic. The British and American S.N. Co. had a ship on order, the *British Queen,* but the Great Western Company had commissioned Isambard Brunel to build the *Great Western,* and it became obvious that this ship would be ready before the *British Queen.* In order to forestall their rivals the British and American Co. chartered the *Sirius* and despatched her from Cork on the 4th April, 1838. It was a desperate and dangerous bid.

With 40 passengers on board, 453 tons of coal and 43 barrels of resin she was grossly overloaded, and had she met heavy weather would almost certainly have foundered. The voyage took 18 days and ten hours, an average speed of 6.7 knots, and 431 tons of coal were consumed. Her triumph, however, was short-lived. Three and a half hours after her arrival the *Great Western* steamed into New York harbour. She had left Avonmouth on 8th April and had taken 15 days, 10½ hours. The Great Western Co. immediately claimed the first official record for the Atlantic crossing—a record that later became known as the 'Blue Riband'.

The third of the trio was the 600-ton *Royal William*, not to be confused with her Canadian namesake, owned by the City of Dublin Steam Packet Company and chartered to the Trans-Atlantic Steamship Company. She left Liverpool on 5th July and took 18 days 23 hours to reach New York. Smaller than both the *Sirius* and the *Great Western* she was the smallest ship ever to steam from Europe to America.

After the heat and fervour of the race to be first had died down the three companies settled down to establishing regular scheduled crossings. The *Great Western* continued to make regular voyages for another seven years, and in 1839 the belated *British Queen* set out on her maiden voyage. She was the largest ship at that time; 182 tons, 275ft long and 64ft across the paddle boxes. Accommodation was provided for 207 passengers, her 500 n.h.p. engines were built by Robert Napier and drove two 30ft diameter paddle-wheels giving her a maximum speed of 10 knots. The journey from Portsmouth to New York took 15 days. She completed two more voyages in that year and five the following year. On the first voyage of 1841 she ran into a severe gale and arrived at Halifax 20 days after leaving Portsmouth. On her return she was sold to the Belgian Government who ran her rather unsuccessfully until 1844 when she was broken up. The owners of the *British Queen* ordered a sister ship in 1838, the 2,350-

ton P.S. *President*. On 1st August, 1840 the ship left Liverpool for New York where she arrived on the 17th. This, and her next voyage, was disappointing in terms of speed, and her third voyage the following year even more so. The passage took twenty-one days, and it was apparent that her engines lacked the power required for so large a ship. On the return trip she left New York on 11th March, 1841, the following afternoon she was sighted labouring heavily in bad weather. She was never seen again. 136 passengers and crew were lost, and it is probable that the inadequacy of her engines was to blame.

By now the advantages of the steamship were being recognised and in November 1838, the Admiralty advertised for tenders for a mail service between Britain and North America by steamship. Samuel Cunard promptly left Novia Scotia for London to apply for the contract. Cunard was a successful merchant living in Halifax. His business interests included timber, whaling and ironfounding. He also owned a fleet of forty coastal sailing ships and had received a contract to deliver mail between Newfoundland, Halifax, Boston and Bermuda.

His part ownership of the *Royal William* gave him the chance to study the potential of the steamship, and when the *Great Western* and *Sirius* proved that Atlantic crossings were possible his interest was further aroused. The Atlantic mails were carried in small brigs. They were slow, often unseaworthy and earned the nickname 'coffin ships'. The unreliability of this service seriously affected Cunard's business, as he could not guarantee dates for the onward shipment of mail. It seemed to him that the answer lay in a regular steamship service, and it was with this in mind that he set out for England.

On his arrival in London, Cunard secured an interview with the Secretary of the Admiralty, and, on 11th February, he undertook to meet the requirements of the Admiralty tender for an annual sum of £55,000.

His next task was to find someone to build his ships. The firm of Wood and Napier were recommended to him, and it was Robert Napier whom Cunard approached. Napier was a brilliant engineer who built and designed marine engines, while hulls were built by his partner, John Wood.

Cunard's original plans were for three ships, which Napier agreed to build. Later he suggested to Cunard that four ships, larger and more powerful than those proposed would be more suitable. To obtain financial backing for the project Napier introduced Cunard to George Burns, a Liverpool ship owner. Burn's agent, David McIver, was also approached and, after some reticence, he agreed to become a partner. With Cunard, Napier, Burns and McIver as principal shareholders the Company was registered as The British and North American Royal Mail Steam Packet Company, a cumbersome title that soon became the Cunard Company.

The four ships were named *Britannia, Acadia, Caledonia* and *Columbia*. All were of the same class, 1,150 tons, 207ft in length by 34ft in breadth. By placing the orders at different yards Cunard ensured quick delivery and *Britannia* sailed on her maiden voyage five months after her launching.

The engines of the *Britannia* and her sister ships were built by Robert Napier. They comprised of a pair of cylinders 6ft in diameter by 6ft 10 inches stroke giving 740 n.p. at 16 revolutions per minute

Napier was responsible for the engines in all the Cunard wooden paddle steamers and later he acquired his own shipyard where he built hulls as well.

The inaugural voyage of the *Britannia* commenced on 4th July, 1840, and took 12 days and 10 hours between Liverpool and Halifax. This time represented the caution of the owners who were not certain of her coal consumption. Her homeward run was completed in 10 days at an

27

average speed of 10 knots. When the *Acadia* joined her
sister ship in August she recorded an average speed of $9\frac{1}{4}$
knots westward and $10\frac{3}{4}$ knots eastwards. *Caledonia* went
into service in October, and *Columbia* in January 1841.

The ships were an immediate success with passengers
and merchants alike. The main deck berthed 115 passengers and 225 tons of cargo could be carried in the hold.
The dining saloon was a long deck-house placed on the
upper deck and there was also a 'ladies only' saloon. The
fare to Halifax was 35 guineas which included wines and
spirits as well as food. Departures from Liverpool took
place on 4th and 19th of each month.

Part of the original contract required provision of a
coastal service between Pictou in Nova Scotia and
Quebec. For this route Cunard used the 650-ton P.S.
Unicorn belonging to George Burns and which was used
by him on his Glasgow-Liverpool run. The *Unicorn* went
to Canada in 1840 and maintained the service until 1846
when arrangements were made to deliver the mail
overland.

After three years, experience had shown that five ships
were required to maintain the schedules, and a new
steamer, the *Hibernia,* was ordered. About the same time
the *Columbia* was lost just outside Halifax and a sister
ship to the *Hibernia,* the *Cambria,* was ordered as a replacement. They were slightly larger than the *Britannia*
class, 1,400 tons and 217ft in length. *Hibernia* averaged
11.67 knots eastwards and the *Cambria* made a 9 day west
to east crossing in 1847.

Between 1848 and 1853 nine more vessels were added
to the fleet. Then in 1856, the first iron-built Cunarder
left the newly-acquired yards of Robert Napier. Nearly
twice the length of *Britannia* and with engines giving five
times the power, the *Persia* dominated all her rivals.

Her speed of 14 knots produced record passage times of
9 days 13 hours 41 minutes westward and 9 days 4 hours

Fig. 3 — P.S. PRESIDENT, sister ship to the BRITISH QUEEN. She was lost in the Atlantic in 1841 with all passengers and crew.

(Photo Science Museum, London).

The Cork Steam Ship Company's

STEAM SHIP

SIRIUS

700 TONS. 320 HORSES POWER.

Fig. 4.—GREAT WESTERN'S rival the SIRIUS.
(Photo Science Museum, London).

45 minutes eastward. She held the Blue Riband from 1856 until 1862.

Despite these record times the competition from screw driven vessels was beginning to have an effect. Although no faster than the paddlers they were more economical and their compact engines allowed for greater passenger and cargo space. In 1862 Cunard took delivery of their last paddle-steamer, the *Scotia*. An improved version of the *Persia*, she was the largest ship afloat, apart from the gigantic *Great Eastern*. Her best crossing, from Cobh, in Ireland, to New York, was 8 days 3 hours and 6 minutes and she took the Blue Riband from her predecessor and held it until 1867. For 13 years she remained in service and when she was withdrawn the days of the ocean paddle steamers came to a close.

Cunard's most serious rival in the early days was Edward Collins, an American who founded the Collins Line in 1849. For some time the American government had been concerned at Cunard's virtual monopoly of the Atlantic trade, and when Collins was awarded a mail contract by Congress he set out to put his British rival out of business. But for tragedy and ill-luck he may well have succeeded.

Four steamships, named *Arctic, Baltic, Atlantic* and *Pacific,* were the nucleus of his fleet. The first to be launched, the *Atlantic,* was 277ft in length, with a gross tonnage of 2,845 and powered by engines of 800 h.p. Her passenger facilities far outclassed her rivals, with bathrooms, barber's shops and smoke-rooms. The maiden voyage took 10 days and 16 hours, clipping 12 hours off the existing Cunard record. When she was joined by her sister ships the battle for the North Atlantic reached its climax. Collins' ships consistently bettered the Cunarders' times and when the *Baltic* became the first mail ship to cross in less than ten days Collins announced that he intended to improve upon this time to eight days.

Cunard came under pressure from the British government to improve his service. To meet the challenge he ordered the *Arabia* but the ship was a disappointing failure.

The fiercely contested battle continued with Collins always getting the edge until the first tragedy struck. Collins had visited Europe with his wife and two children on several occasions. On September 21st, 1854, the *Arctic* left Liverpool with 233 passengers, including Mrs. Collins and the two children. The weather was fair until the ship was not more than sixty miles from home. Then, in thick fog, she was run down by a French vessel and holed in three places. At the moment of impact the *Arctic* had been steaming at full speed, as she always did. With no watertight compartments the vessel filled quickly and the race was on to reach land. Only fifteen miles out and with land in sight the *Arctic* rolled over and went down taking all but eighty survivors with her. The next day Collins went to meet his ship and his family; instead he received a letter from the captain, who had been rescued and was in hospital, informing him of the death of his wife, son and daughter.

The grief stricken Collins could well have lost interest in the company at this point. Instead, he planned a floating memorial to his wife, the largest, fastest and most luxurious ship the world had ever seen. The *Adriatic*.

But the unkind fate that had struck him such a cruel blow was still not finished with him. Twelve months after the loss of the *Arctic,* the *Pacific* disappeared without trace. What happened to her was never known. It is probable that she hit an iceberg and if, as seems likely, she was steaming at full speed then she would have foundered immediately.

Collins, however, still refused to despair. The *Persia* was winning back the Cunard supremacy, but he was convinced that the *Adriatic* would redress the balance.

Her gross tonnage was 3,670 and she had a maximum speed of 13 knots compared with the *Persia*'s 12½ knots. Then politics took a hand. America was on the verge of civil war. Collins lost the mail contract because of a Bill forced through Congress by the South, and a few months later the Collins Line went into liquidation.

The *Adriatic* had only been in service a few months but during that time she fulfilled Collins' cherished ambition.

Her maiden voyage took ten days and she was one-third less costly to operate than the *Persia*. Her most amazing voyage was in the service of her new owners, the Galway Line, when she crossed from Galway to New-foundland in 5 days 19¾ hours.

The collapse of the Collins Line left Cunard with very little opposition. The Transatlantic Company had merged with P & O in 1840, the British and American S.N. Company was also shortlived and the Great Western Company had retired from the field in 1846.

The battle for the Atlantic trade had all the glamour and publicity of a heavy-weight prize fight, but on the other oceans the steamship was opening up new services in less spectacular fashion. In 1825 the first England to India passage was made by the tiny *Enterprise,* a wooden paddler 122ft in length with engines of 120 n.h.p. The voyage was a bid to win the £8,000 prize offered by the Calcutta 'Steam Committee' for a steamship that could cover the distance in seventy days. The *Enterprise* failed to meet these conditions as she took 113 days, but she was awarded half the prize money. Later the ship was bought by the Government of Bengal.

The greatest inducement to steamship companies was the award of a government mail contract. Following the introduction of the Atlantic mail service by Cunard, the Admiralty advertised a similar contract for the service to Egypt. Four tenders were placed and the contract was won by the Peninsular Steam Navigation Company, who undertook to make one passage each month via Malta. The company had been in existence for many years, trading to the Iberian peninsular ports of Malaga, Oporto and Gibraltar. When the new contract was obtained the company added 'Orient' to its title to encompass the eastward route. The Peninsular and Orient Steam Navigation Company soon became known as the P & O—a name that was to become as famous as Cunard.

The route to Egypt was later extended to include India, and some early vessels on this service were the *Great Liverpool, Hindustan, Bentinck* and *Oriental*. They were all wooden built vessels with a speed of about 9 knots. The *Oriental,* on one occasion, logged 2,880 miles between Alexandria and Falmouth which she covered in $314\frac{1}{2}$ hours.

Unlike Cunard the P & O recognised the value of screw ships early on, and their fleet consisted of a mixture of both types for many years. The last P & O paddler was the *Nyanza,* an iron built vessel launched in 1864 and fitted with oscillating engines. She was withdrawn from service in 1873 and was sold to the Union Line who converted her to screw propulsion. Later she became the private yacht of the Sultan of Zanzibar.

And so the ocean paddle steamers made way for progress. Much of their popularity had been due to the fact that their passengers believed what they could see, and the sight of those huge paddle-wheels thrusting the vessel forward was very reassuring. They were rugged ships, pitting their often puny engines against the power of the open seas. Disasters there were, but relatively few considering the hard and often reckless way in which they were driven. Commercially they were never successful. Many ended their days as pure sailing ships, some were converted to screw propulsion, others to coal hulks, but they hold a glorious place in the history of marine steam navigation.

Chapter Three

THE 'GREAT WESTERN'

Brunel's idea — The Great Western Steamship Company —
Misfortunes and triumphs.

THE formation of the Great Western Steamship Company was inspired by the chief engineer of the G.W.R.,
Isambard Kingdom Brunel. Brunel was a man of genius
and great enterprise. From Paddington Station in London
to Temple Meads in Bristol his bridges, tunnels and cut-
tings made possible the railway that was to become
famous for its speed, safety and reliability. But before the
line was completed Brunel turned his attention to
steamships.

From childhood he had been interested in ships, and
his enthusiasm for steam was inherited from his father.
Marc Brunel had first experimented with steamships on
the Thames in 1814 and several patents were taken out in
his name. These included a surface condenser to overcome the need to use sea-water in boilers, and a mechanical stoker. Yet he did not believe that an ocean-going
steamship was feasible. Many engineers of the time argued
that no ship could carry enough coal for an Atlantic
voyage.

If you double the size of the hull, they said, then
you need twice the power to drive it through the water
and therefore twice the amount of coal. The argument

seemed logical, but Brunel never accepted the logic of others without question. He looked for the flaw in the argument, which was quite simply that increasing the hull size, and therefore the capacity, does not increase its resistance in the water by the same amount. Having established that fact it only remained to find someone to back up his idea.

The opportunity came at a meeting of the board of the Great Western Railway Company in 1835. Some members expressed their concern at the length of the proposed line from London to Bristol. Brunel countered their doubts with the suggestion that the line could be lengthened even further—to New York. To the assembled directors this remark was absurd, and was dismissed as a joke. But one man, Thomas Guppy, knew that Brunel was serious, and as soon as the meeting was over he asked the engineer to explain his proposal.

Brunel had a persuasive personality, his idea of a transatlantic steamship captured Guppy's imagination and the outcome of the meeting was the formation of the Great Western Steamship Company. The Chairman of the Company was Peter Maze of the G.W.R. and the Managing Director was Christopher Claxton, a close friend of Brunel.

Work on the ship commenced in July 1836. The building contract was placed with William Patterson of Bristol, under the supervision of a committee consisting of Brunel, Claxton and Guppy. Brunel's work kept him in London for most of the time, but whenever he was in Bristol he would visit his brainchild and took a great interest in its progress. He had insisted from the start that strength should be a major factor in the design of the hull. The traditional English oak was used and the framework was based on the principle used in the construction of ships of the Royal Navy.

The overall length of the hull was 236ft. The breadth

was 35.3ft, extending to 59.8ft over the paddle-boxes, and the draught was 16.7ft.

To drive a ship of that size, larger than any steamship then afloat, required engines of unprecedented power. The most experienced marine engine builders were Maudslay Sons and Field Ltd., of Blackwall, and on Brunel's advice this Company was given the contract. The specification required engines capable of providing 750 I.H.P. and this was achieved with a side-lever, twin cylinder engine working at a steam pressure of 5 pounds per square inch. Each cylinder could drive one paddle-wheel independently, or both together, which accounts for the plural term 'engines' when applied to a single unit. The diameter of the cylinders was 73.5 inches, and the stroke was 7ft. The engines revolved at a speed of 15 revolutions per minute, giving a nominal horsepower of 450 at the paddle-wheels which were 28.75ft in diameter.

On July 19th, 1837, the *Great Western* left her dry dock and moved out into Bristol harbour. A celebration lunch was held in the main saloon and a month later the ship sailed to Blackwall to receive her engines.

Her arrival in the Thames was greeted with considerable public interest. The press were unanimous in their admiration for her smart lines and impressive size. And impressive she must have been. The hull was painted all black and a gilded figure of Neptune, flanked by two dolphins, decorated the graceful prow.

Not the least of her wonders was the Main Saloon. This was placed on the main deck and was 75ft long. The width of the room for most of its length was 21ft but in places there were recesses that extended the width to 34ft. Although the press made rapturous comments on the decor no pictures or graphic descriptions seem to have survived. But there are many examples of Victorian elegance from which we can draw a mental picture. The saloon was, in effect, a floating drawing-room, and would therefore have been decorated in the manner of such rooms. Ornate columns to support the 9ft high ceiling, elaborate cornice work and polished brass oil-lamps.

The walls were probably decorated with paintings depicting the origin and role of the ship, and everywhere there would be huge mirrors set in gilt frames. The furniture would have been comfortable, and upholstered in the rich-red plush so beloved by the Victorians. Amidst all this splendour passengers could while away the long hours of the voyage, and talk about the marvels of modern travel over tea served in bone-china teacups.

While the people of London marvelled at the new ship, others viewed her with jealous eyes. London and Liverpool were the major British ports, and the *Great Western* was a Bristolian. Her fitting-out was taking place right under the nose of the British and American Steam Navigation Company, a London firm whose chartered vessel, the *Sirius,* was also on the Thames being prepared for her Atlantic crossing. Work on the *Great Western* was stepped up to get her back to Bristol for her maiden voyage, but on March 28th, 1838, the *Sirius* moved down the river on the first leg of her momentous voyage. Three days later the *Great Western* set off in pursuit of her rival. On board were Brunel, Guppy and Claxton.

Despite the gap between the two ships Brunel was not despondent. He knew that the *Sirius* would be stopping at Cork for refuelliing and he was confident that his ship could get to Bristol and leave again before the *Sirius* started on the crossing. His confidence was soon to be shattered. Only two hours after leaving London the *Great Western* was suddenly enveloped in a thick cloud of smoke. Flames engulfed the forward boiler room and rapidly spread to the deck. Prompt action by the Chief Engineer, George Pearne, prevented a boiler explosion and Claxton went below to help fight the flames.

Brunel started to descend into the boiler room, but the

36

Fig. 5 — Brunel's masterpiece, the GREAT WESTERN, forerunner of the modern ocean liner.
(Photo Science Museum, London).

Fig. 6 — Brunel's great ship, the GREAT EASTERN. Her designer did not live to see her maiden voyage.

(Photo Science Museum, London)

flames had already spread to the ladder and it collapsed under his weight. Claxton was standing at the foot of the ladder and received the full force of Brunel's fall. His presence undoubtedly saved Brunel from serious injury.

In the meantime Lieutenant James Hosken, R.N., captain of the *Great Western,* had steered his ship towards Canvey Island where she went aground. Brunel was in great pain and had to be put ashore, where he remained for several weeks.

The fire had been caused by the spontaneous combustion of the boiler lagging, which had been taken too close to the furnace flues. Although the damage was extensive, the ship sailed on the next tide to continue her voyage to Bristol. Good progress was made and she arrived at Bristol on April 2nd. Brunel's injuries did not prevent him from drawing up a list of matters to be attended to before the ship sailed again, and once these were received, Claxton set about preparing for the voyage to New York.

The sailing date was fixed for April 7th, but bad weather delayed the start, so that it was at 10 a.m. on April 8th that the *Great Western* left her home port in the now hopeless pursuit of her rival.

The voyage was uneventful. After the near disastrous incident at Canvey Island the ship settled down to prove all of Brunel's theories. She steamed at an average speed of 8.8 knots and gained on the *Sirius* at the rate of two knots per hour. On one day she covered 243 miles. The engines never missed a beat, and 15 days 5 hours after leaving England the *Great Western* anchored outside New York harbour in the early hours of the morning.

New Yorkers had hardly finished celebrating the arrival of the *Sirius* before the *Great Western* made her triumphant entry into the harbour. It was a clear day and the crowds had gathered to every vantage point to witness this second historic occasion. Lieutenant Hosken, having achieved all that he had set out to do, permitted himself a little showmanship. As the *Great Western* approached the *Sirius* at her moorings she slowed perceptibly, then turned in a half circle to show off her beautiful lines to the enthusiastic crowd.

This coquettish display over, Hosken ordered full speed ahead to demonstrate the ship's superior speed, a manoeuvre that brought wild cheers from the onlookers. But below deck yet another tragedy was about to take place. George Pearne, the man who had saved the ship from destruction was on duty. As the *Great Western* moved into her berth he started to clear the boilers. There was a sudden rush of steam and Pearne was fatally scalded.

Although the *Sirius* had won the distinction of being the first steamer to cross the Atlantic her voyage had done nothing to show that a regular transatlantic service was possible. The *Great Western,* on the other hand, had set a new standard in speed, comfort and reliability, and the Great Western Steamship Company's claim for the official record made sure that everyone was aware of the importance of the achievement. Certainly the Americans were impressed, for when the ship left New York to return to Bristol, 68 passengers were on board

The eastward journey took 15 days, despite a broken connecting rod which put one engine out of action for 48 hours. The ship arrived in Bristol on May 22nd, 1838, amid scenes of great rejoicing. The first round of the battle between the city and her rivals had been won and it seemed certain that the ancient seaport was about to regain its maritime supremacy.

The *Great Western* continued to make regular crossings, and in 1839 the battle with the British and American Steamship Company was joined once again. Their ship, the *British Queen,* was due to leave New York on August 1st, and the *Great Western* was also scheduled to leave on the same day. It was known that the *Great Western* could steam at an average speed of 8.8 knots, against her rival's 8.4 knots, and the trial of strength between the two vessels was watched with great interest. As it turned out it was the strength of Brunel's ship that won the day.

She was superior to the *British Queen* in rough weather, and docked in Bristol in the evening of August 14th. The *British Queen* arrived at Portsmouth the following morning.

For eight years the *Great Western* shuttled between Bristol and New York. Sixty-seven trips were made during that period, regardless of the weather, and her times were often better than the mail steamers which used the shorter route to Halifax.

The feasibility of an Atlantic steamship had been proved. Brunel began to make plans for a larger and better ship. The result was the famous screw ship *Great Britain*. Much of what Brunel had learnt with the *Great Western* went into the design of the new ship, which was originally intended to be paddle driven. But the delays caused by Brunel's new obsession with the propellor caused the Company to suffer financially.

One ship alone could not be commercially successful, and by the time the *Great Britain* was launched in 1843 the Company's finances were perilously low. A series of mishaps to the new ship further weakened their position and in 1847 the Great Western Steamship Company, owners of two of the most remarkable ships ever built, went out of business. The *Great Western* was sold to the Royal Mail Steam Packet Company who she served for ten years with the same unflagging dependability she had given her first owners. In 1856 she was broken up at Millbank, and Brunel himself visited her to pay his last respects.

Chapter Four

PADDLE STEAMERS OF THE THAMES AND MEDWAY

Opposition of the Watermen — Fierce competition — Luxury vessels develop — Belle Steamers — Palace Steamers — Woolwich Ferries — Medway 'Queens' — General Steam Navigation Company survive competition.

WHILE the giant paddlers were fighting a losing battle on the high seas their little sisters were doing very well on the inland and coastal waters of Britain. The most important waterway in Britain is the river Thames, and, inevitably, the paddle steamers became part of the river scene very early in their history. The *Margery* and *Thames,* (see Chapter One), were built only two years after the *Comet* had shown that the steamboat was a practical proposition. During the following years, until the turn of the century, their numbers increased rapidly and at one time fifteen companies were operating on the river.

The early river steamers were not a success. Breakdowns were frequent, machinery was expensive to maintain and fierce opposition was encountered from the Watermen. Prior to the introduction of the steamboats, the Watermen had operated ferry services between London and Gravesend using large rowing boats, known as 'tilt' boats. Attempts to thwart the new steamboats ranged from deliberate obstruction to sabotage, but the outcome was inevitable and the last 'tilt' boat was withdrawn in 1834.

Until the 1820's steamer services were confined to the

London to Gravesend run and to the estuary towns such as Margate, Southend and Ramsgate. As confidence in the vessels grew the routes were extended to Calais and Boulogne, but no Thames paddle steamer ever equalled the remarkable journey of the *Sophia Jane*. Built in 1826 by Barnes and Miller at Ratcliffe, for the London-Margate run, she also ran between London and Calais and, under the ownership of the St. George Steam Packet Company, between Liverpool and Douglas. The *Sophia Jane* was 126ft by 20ft with a burden of 256 tons. Her engines produced a mere 50 n.h.p., yet when she was purchased by a Sydney firm, she steamed to Australia, to become that country's first steamship, and the first to steam from Britain to Australia. She arrived in Sydney on May 16th, 1831, and operated along the Australian coast until 1845.

When the Watermen realised that physical opposition to the steamers was futile, they adopted a principle of, 'if you can't beat 'em, join 'em'.

In 1840 they formed the Waterman's Steam Packet Company with a fleet of twelve fast packets. Their strongest rival at that time was the Woolwich Steam Packet Company who had borne the brunt of the Watermen's opposition. Now, with their new fleet, the Watermen set out to beat their competitors at their own game. The packets were deliberately timed to start together and racing was indulged in with no regard for the safety of the vessels, their passengers or other river craft.

It was the Waterman's Company, however, that eventually found the pace too hot. They gave up the contest and, in 1865, were bought out by their erstwhile rivals.

With the addition of twelve boats to their fleet the Woolwich Company were able to provide a service strong enough to resist the competition of the railways when the line was extended to North Woolwich. Their fleet was the largest operating on the Thames and they had the monopoly of passenger traffic from Richmond down to Southend. The first saloon steamer, the *Alexandria*, was put into service by the Woolwich Company.

She was built in Glasgow in 1865 for use as a blockade-runner in the American Civil War, but that conflict ended before the ship was completed and she lived a more peaceful existence on London's river for ten years. The ship could carry 1,048 passengers and the fares from London to Gravesend in the two deck saloons were one shilling in the Fore Saloon and one shilling and sixpence in the Grand Saloon. Another Woolwich steamer, the *Sybil*, was the victim of an unfortunate incident in 1863 while H.R.H. Princess Alexandria was visiting London. During the excitement of the occasion the vessel struck an object just below London Bridge and sank immediately. The ship was crowded with sightseers at the time but all were safely rescued.

Despite its monopoly and enormous success the Woolwich Steam Pack Company survived for only ten years. Its successor, the London Steamboat Company, was founded at a time when it would have seemed impossible not to succeed.

The paddle steamers had, by now, thoroughly established themselves as a cheap, reliable form of transport and thousands of Londoners used them daily. With the fleet of the Woolwich Company and the small Citizens Company, which they had also acquired, they had seventy boats working on the river. Yet the Company constantly ran at a loss, and when they were hit by the terrible disaster of the *Princess Alice,* (see Chapter Six), they never recovered. In 1884 the boats were offered for sale by auction and the entire fleet was taken over by a new company the River Thames Steamboat Company. This Company had little more success than its predecessors and two years later the fleet was again up for sale. There were no takers and the Company sold 14 vessels for breaking. They continued to operate with the remaining boats until 1890 when they went into liquidation and the assets were picked up by the Victoria Steamboat Association. This company was also shortlived and in 1897 yet another concern, the Thames Steamboat Company, took over the remnants of the fleet, and at the same time they ordered three new vessels.

Named *Alexandra, Boadicea* and *Cleopatra,* they became known as the 'A.B.C.' ships. They were fine ships and gave an excellent service, but the company failed to make them pay and after five years they too were forced to close down.

In 1887 the Clacton Pier Company refused permission for the River Thames Company to land there, owing to non-payment of landing fees. This had an adverse effect on the town's holiday trade and so it was decided to form a company to be known as the London, Woolwich and Clacton-on-Sea Steamship Company, in which the Pier Company were the chief shareholders. Their first boat, the *Clacton,* was superior to any of the River Thames Company's vessels. She had a saloon on the upper deck, with a dining saloon below. Compound engines of 204 n.h.p. were fitted and over a measured mile the ship achieved a speed of 16 knots. After only one season the *Clacton* was sold to Turkey where she was renamed *Aidin.* The Company dropped out of the steamboat business for two years and then re-started with a fleet of four vessels built over a period of six years.

Each ship was given the title 'Belle' in its name, *Clacton Belle, Woolwich Belle, London Belle* and *Southend Belle.* The Company was reconstituted as Belle Steamers Ltd., in 1897 and added three more 'Belles' to their fleet, the *Walton Belle, Yarmouth Belle* and *Southwold Belle.*

The 'Belle' steamers were very popular with holiday-

43

makers. Each vessel had different characteristics with varying saloon arrangements. In appearance they differed from other boats on the Thames; one unusual feature being that the bridge was placed aft of the funnel. At the start of the First World War trading ceased and the boats were taken over by the Admiralty. After the war they continued in the service of various companies, some of them changing hands several times. The *Southend Belle* had the most chequered career of all. After her war service she passed through the hands of several owners, during which time she was renamed *Laguna Belle*. In the 1930's she was the only paddle steamer to run from London to Clacton direct, and the author recalls such a trip in extremely rough weather which did nothing to endear him to paddle steamers at that time.

During the Second World War she was again taken over by the Admiralty and was one of the few paddle steamers to serve in both wars.

The latter part of the nineteenth century marked the heyday of the paddle steamer. The Estuary and Kent coast resorts boomed with the trade brought to them by the fleets of pleasure steamers that arrived daily during the summer season. A trip to Margate or Clacton was the Londoner's favourite way of spending a day out. But in order to make the most of the day, trippers demanded a fast and comfortable journey, and no company offered a service that could compete with that of the Palace Steamers. Palace Steamers Limited comprised only three ships, but what ships they were. The *Koh-I-Noor, Royal Sovereign* and *La Marguerite* were the largest, fastest and most luxurious paddle steamers on the Thames. The *Koh-I-Noor*, of 884 tons, was built by the Fairfield Shipbuilding and Engineering Company at a cost of £50,000. During her trials she covered the measured mile at a mean speed of 19.499 knots. She was constructed of steel and was 300.4ft long and 58ft broad over the paddle-boxes.

Fig. 7 — General Steam Navigation Company's **P.S. LAVEROCK.**
(Photo Science Museum, London).

Fig. 8—P.S. GOLDEN EAGLE. (Photo courtesy of Southern Ferries).

Fig. 9—P.S. MEDWAY QUEEN. (Photo courtesy of Southern Ferries.)

Fig. 10 — New Medway Steam Packet Company's QUEEN OF KENT at Southend Pier.   (Photo courtesy of Southern Ferries).

Engines giving an indicated horsepower of 3,500 were fitted. They were twin cylinder diagonal compound, the high pressure cylinder being 45 inches in diameter and the low pressure 80 inches, with a stroke of 66 inches.

The two funnels were telescopic to allow for passage under London Bridge and the mast was hinged for the same purpose. The hull was divided into watertight compartments and the main deck had two saloons which supported a promenade deck running almost the entire length of the boat. Passenger facilities were of the nature of a small liner. A first class dining saloon, spacious second class saloon, post office, hairdressing establishment, two bathrooms, book and fruit stalls, and a complete electric lighting system. The *Koh-I-Noor* made a near disastrous start when she left the builder's yards on the Clyde in 1892. Making her way down the Welsh coast in dense fog she stranded near St. Davids Head, severely damaging the bow. Inspection revealed that the damage extended nearly twenty feet along the side and after temporary repairs she returned to the builders where a new bow was fitted.

Once her service commenced, however, she was extremely popular, as was her sister the *Royal Sovereign*. The second of the Palace Steamers, the *Royal Sovereign,* was almost identical to the *Koh-I-Noor* with the exception of her funnels which were set slightly further apart. The same excellent facilities were provided, plus a deck bar forward of the funnels. The third ship of the trio, the *La Marguerite,* was the largest paddle steamer on the Thames up to that time. Built by the same Company as her two companions her gross tonnage was 1,544, and she had engines of 7,500 indicated horsepower giving her a speed of 20 knots. It was intended to employ the ship on the London to Boulogne service, but her speed and size were too great to meet the requirements of the Thames

Conservancy Board and she had to depart from Tilbury. This was the first time that the public were able to travel to Boulogne and return on the same day. In spite of its popularity the ship was costly to run and it never showed a profit.

Nevertheless, she ran for ten seasons, the Company obviously valuing the prestige she brought enough to overlook the high running costs. In 1904 the *La Marguerite* left the Thames to operate on the North Wales coast under the ownership of the Liverpool and North Wales Steamship Company.

For some time the London County Council had been proposing that it should run its own steamboat service. This required an Act of Parliament and in 1904 a Bill was passed. The L.C.C. immediately ordered thirty boats at a cost of £6,000 each. Ten were built by Thornycroft, ten by Napier and Miller and ten by the Thames Iron Works. They were all about the same size, varying between 116 to 126 tons, and carried 500 passengers. At first the Council suffered from a lack of expert advice until the fleet was put under the control of Captain Arthur Owen. He had been master of the *La Marguerite* and his experience soon resulted in an efficient service. Unfortunately the L.C.C. ruined its chances of success by competing with itself. Their elaborate tramway system took custom away from the steamers and they were withdrawn in 1907.

Joining the Thames at its estuary is the river Medway, a navigable waterway of some twenty miles. Prior to the advent of the railway, a steamer service linking Chatham and Sheerness was started in 1837 by the Medway Steam Packet Company. Some of the Company's vessels were built on the Medway and although there is little record of the earlier boats, it is known that many of them were constructed of mahogany. None of the Medway Steamers were very big, the *City of Rochester II*, at 235 tons, being one of the largest. During the First World War she carried troops to the block ships that took part in the famous raid on Zeebrugge.

In 1924 the Company adopted the slogan 'The Queen line of steamers' and in that year ordered their first 'Queen', the *Medway Queen*. Her tonnage was 318 gross and she had a speed of 15 knots. Dimensions were 179.9ft by 24.2ft and the compound diagonal engines had a nominal horsepower of 76. The vessel operated on the Rochester to Southend service, and also the Herne Bay service.

She was a workaday ship that was to earn battle honours in the Second World War and become the object of considerable public interest after the war.

The fleet of 'Queen' steamers was extended by the purchase of several vessels from other companies, including three of the 'Belle' steamers. Thus the *Woolwich Belle* became the *Queen of the South,* in 1925 the *Walton Belle* became *Essex Queen* and in 1928 the *Yarmouth Belle* became the *Queen of Southend*. In 1946 the *Walton Belle/Essex Queen* underwent another change of name when she was sold to the South Western Steam Navigation Company and renamed *Pride of Devon*.

Until the late 1840's ferry services across the Thames below London Bridge were operated by the Watermen, using rowing boats. On the north side of the river the Eastern Counties Railway terminated at Fenchurch Street and Liverpool Street, and a faster link between the north and south banks was required.

The railway company started a ferry service using two paddle steamers which were timed to coincide with the arrival and departure of trains at the two stations.

The expected antagonism from the Watermen was avoided by employing them as masters and mates of the steamers. The fare in each direction was one penny, but in 1890 the London County Council opened a free service alongside the railway ferry, and this became known as the

Woolwich Free Ferry. Unable to compete with this, the Eastern Railway ferry closed down in 1908.

The Woolwich Ferry paddle steamers had none of the elegance of the excursion steamers. They were functional vessels built to transport passengers and vehicles across the fast-flowing river, and these requirements dictated their design. Two engines drove each paddle-wheel independently, and the vessels could reach a speed of 8 knots when both engines were driving full ahead. Most of the time, however, the journey was made in a series of short bursts from each paddle-wheel in turn as the ferry left or approached the landing stage.

The Woolwich Free Ferry was, and still is, as much a part of London Life as coffee-stalls and costermonger's barrows. Three vessels originally ran between the two stages, the *Gordon, Duncan* and *Hutton.* Later they were replaced by the *Squires, John Benn, Will Crooks* and another *Gordon.* Running at nine minute intervals from dawn until midnight they continued until 1963 when they were replaced by diesel-driven vessels. Their passing was mourned by regular users who had come to look upon them with great affection, and they were among the last paddle steamers to be seen on the Thames.

Just before the First World War there were signs that the days of the paddle steamer as a regular passenger service vehicle were coming to an end. The Thames is not an ideal highway for a public transport system. Its looping bends can more than double the distance between points, and as the railway, tramway, omnibus and underground systems were developed so the river services began to lose trade.

The paddle steamers were used less and less as packets and began to fall back on the pleasure excursion trade. After the war they had to compete with a new rival. The char-a-banc. The char-a-banc trips took Londoners out of the smoky environment of the town and into the country lanes of the Home Counties. Southend, Margate, and Clacton could be reached much more quickly, and there was new scenery to be viewed en route.

The steamship companies suffered badly. Few had survived the competition of the earlier days and those that had were the results of mergers. One attempt to win back customers to the river was the *Showboat*. The ex-South coast paddle steamer *Alexandra* was purchased by a London syndicate and converted to a luxury floating restaurant and dance hall. Evening cruises from West-minster Pier down river, with dinner, dancing and a cabaret, were followed by a supper cruise up river. It was a novel idea, but a failure. The year was 1932, hardly the time to persuade people to spend money on such extravagances.

After one season the *Alexandra* was towed to Margate where she was used as a dance hall. Later that year she moved to Shoreham where her attractions were available to Brighton holidaymakers, and in 1934 she was towed to a breakers. But at least the *Showboat* had offered some-thing different in the way of entertainment on the Thames, and nothing like it has been seen until the *Princess Elizabeth* opened in 1971.

By 1939 only a handful of paddle steamers were running pleasure excursions to the Kent and Essex resorts. The char-a-banc had become the luxury motor coach, and the private motor-car was giving people an independent means of travel. The few remaining paddle steamers were owned by a company that had started in 1824, had survived all the competition and take-overs, and had provided some of the finest and most popular steamers on the river. This was the General Steam Navigation Company.

Chapter Five

THE 'NAVVIES'

THE General Steam Navigation Company can claim to
be the oldest steamship company in the world. The other
claimant to the title, the Clyde Shipping Company of
1819, operated only river steamers, whereas the G.S.N.
was founded with the express intention of operating on
the world trade routes.

Certainly it is the oldest in existence, for it was in 1824
that a small group of steamship owners banded together
for the purpose of developing steam navigation.

It was a daring, ambitious venture as the steamship was
still in its infancy, and there were many who were convinced that it had no future. The main argument against
it was that sailing ships used the natural, and free,
elements of the winds whereas steam had to be paid for.
They conveniently forgot that nature can be very contrary, sometimes providing too much wind and sometimes
none at all.

The men who believed in steam needed the courage of
their convictions. Two such men were William John Hall
and Thomas Brocklebank. Hall was a shipowner whose
vessels traded between London and Hull. Brocklebank
was a timber merchant who had built a small steam

packet, the *Eagle,* in his yard at Deptford in 1820. Together they decided to form a Joint-Stock Company to be known as the General Steam Navigation Company.

At a meeting held on 20th June, 1824, the Company declared its intention to trade with various countries including India, North and South America, Portugal, Spain, France, Holland and Russia. This ambitious programme was later modified to cover what is known as the Home Trade, that is the ports lying between Hamburg and Brest. After a few years the Mediterranean was included. What may have been a defiant gesture to their critics was a proposal to station vessels around the coast to give assistance to sailing ships affected by contrary winds.

It is interesting to note that the G.S.N. was founded one year before the first railway, the Stockton to Darlington, was opened. The steam locomotive and the marine steam engine were developed at about the same time, but the railways needed tracks to run on whereas the steamships used the oldest highway in the world. Consequently the steamships were well established before the railways were able to offer a comparable service.

Seven steam packets made up the Thames fleet of the G.S.N. in 1824. Brocklebank's *Eagle* of 170 tons, the *Venus,* 202 tons, *Royal Sovereign,* 220 tons, *City of London,* 185 tons, *Hero,* 233 tons, *Brocklebank,* 125 tons and the *Eclipse,* 88 tons. The packets ran from London to Margate daily, leaving London at nine o'clock each morning, and to Ramsgate on Wednesdays and Saturdays. There was also a cross-channel service to Boulogne, Calais, and Ostend from London, and one from Brighton to Dieppe. The Brighton service operated from the Chain Pier which was built on the suspension principle. It was destroyed during a fierce gale in 1896.

The journey was advertised as taking eight hours, carriages were transported at £1.1.0. per wheel, horses at £3.3.0. each and dogs at 5s. 0d. each. The longer routes to Lisbon and Gibraltar, Hamburg and Rotterdam were served by the larger steam packets such as the *George The Fourth* and the *Duke of York*, both of 760 tons.

In addition to the passenger services the Company traded in cargo and mail. Live cattle were carried from the Continent to London, until this traffic was prohibited in 1891. But in the early days the Company had no wharf of its own. Passengers embarked and disembarked at the St. Katharine Wharf, and in 1849 a lease was obtained for the St Katharine's Steam Wharf. The dock was one of the most modern of its time, designed so that ships could unload their cargoes directly into the warehouse. Today the St. Katharine Dock is the site of a gigantic development scheme, and the old basin is being retained as a yacht marina.

The fleet of sea-going steamers owned by G.S.N. were among the most elegant of their day. Smaller than the big paddlers that were pioneering the ocean trade routes the 'Navvies' still had the slim, graceful lines of the sailing ships. Beautiful ships with beautiful names, *Waterwitch, Neptune, Rainbow*, their first iron paddler, and *Trident*.

Royal recognition was given to the Company in 1842. The London to Edinburgh service was operated by a fleet of fast packets including the *Trident*. The *Trident* was a wooden paddler of 971 tons and was fitted with engines of 280 n.h.p. She was schooner rigged with three topgallant masts and had a tall single funnel. When it was announced that Queen Victoria intended to journey to Scotland by sea, the Directors of G.S.N. immediately offered the services of any of the Company's vessels. The offer was graciously declined, as arrangements had been made for the Queen and Prince Albert to travel in the Royal Yacht. On the return trip, however, the young Queen expressed the desire to travel in the Company's splendid vessel, the *Trident*.

An account of the voyage is recorded in the Queen's

book 'Leaves from the Journal of our Life in the Highlands'. Her Majesty was particularly pleased with the accommodation which, she said, was superior to that in the *Royal George,* the Royal Yacht, and commented upon the speed of the ship. It is probable that this was the first time that an English monarch had travelled in a privately owned ship.

On the Thames the G.S.N. steamers were very popular, but to maintain that popularity the Company had to keep one jump ahead of their rivals at all times, and it was their ability to do this which kept them as the major steamship operator on the river.

By 1828 the Thames fleet had been increased to twelve, and these boats ran in competition with the many rival concerns that appeared during the next two decades. In 1848 the *Albion* was built, with engines constructed by G.S.N. at their Deptford Works, and the following year the *Prince of Wales* was purchased from the Margate Steam Packet Company.

Of all the paddle steamers to run on the Thames the most famous were the G.S.N.'s *'Eagle'* steamers. Thomas Brocklebank's boat of that name was the first vessel owned by the Company and the name was perpetuated throughout the years. In 1856 the second *Eagle* made her appearance. Much larger than her predecessor, she was licensed to carry 466 passengers to Dover. *Eagle II* was 200ft long and 24ft in breadth, her gross tonnage was 325. Her side-lever engines of 130 n.h.p., built by G.S.N., drove 16ft diameter paddle-wheels each having twelve feathering floats, which gave her a speed of $14\frac{1}{2}$ knots. A smart appearance was always a feature of all G.S.N. boats and the *Eagle* was no exception. The white paddle-boxes, red wheels and deep blue lifeboats contrasted sharply with the black funnel and hull. The figurehead of an eagle adorned the bow and was surrounded by gold filigree. She had no deck saloon, being

53

open from stem to stern, and it was not until 1873 that the Company introduced a ship with this refinement. This was the *Hoboken,* built by Robert Napier at Glasgow.

The *Hoboken* had two deck saloons placed fore and aft of the funnel and topped by a promenade deck. She ran on the Thanet service in conjunction with the *Eagle* and the *Hilda,* a two-funnelled steamer purchased in 1868. The *Hilda* had started life in 1862 as the *Eugenie* on the South Eastern Railway's Continental service from Folkestone to Boulogne. In 1864 she was sold to America and crossed the Atlantic to become a blockade runner. On her return to England the G.S.N. bought and renamed the ship. She closely resembled the *Eagle,* except for her extra funnel, and was the only two-funnelled paddle steamer the Company ever owned apart from the *Royal Sovereign* of 1929.

Another fourteen years passed before the Company considered extending its fleet again. By now the G.S.N. was well established on the river and most of its competitors had fallen by the wayside. Nevertheless, complacency was never one of their failings and, when it was learned that other interests were planning to build faster boats, five new vessels were ordered.

The first of these, the *Halcyon,* was the Company's first steel paddle steamer. During the next two years the other four left the builder's yards. They were the *Mavis, Oriole, Laverock* and *Philomel.* All were around 500 tons gross with compound diagonal engines giving a speed of 17 knots. The new boats were employed on the route to the Kent resorts, and a new service to Great Yarmouth was introduced.

Thus the Company staved off the threatened competition, but only for a few years. As the nineteenth century drew to a close fresh attempts were made to break their monopoly, and in 1898 the Company decided to build another *Eagle.*

The order was placed with Gourley Brothers of Dundee. *Eagle III* was 265ft long, 30ft in breadth, and had a gross tonnage of 647. Engines of 316 n.h.p. were fitted and she had a speed of 18 knots. She operated regularly until 1928, apart from the war years when she was taken over by the Admiralty and named *Aiglon*. In 1929 she was sold for breaking to a Dutch firm and her hull was converted into a landing stage on the River Maas.

In the summer of 1909 there was a new addition to the Thames fleet which was a big advance on all the previous vessels. The *Golden Eagle,* 793 gross tons, 275.7ft long and 32.1ft in breadth. Triple expansion engines of 455 n.h.p. were fitted giving her a speed of 18 knots. She operated daily on the Margate and Ramsgate run with occasional trips to Boulogne. The *Golden Eagle* served in, and survived, both world wars. She restarted her peace-time operations in 1948 and was sold for breaking to British Iron and Steel in 1952.

By 1925 the excursion trade was firmly in the hands of the Company, but in that year they decided to build what was probably their finest paddle steamer ever. The *Crested Eagle* was built at Cowes by J. Samuel White and Company. She was 299ft in length and over 1,000 tons gross. The hull was divided into ten watertight compartments and the promenade deck ran from the bow to within a few feet of the stern. The first class dining saloon, which was situated forward on the main deck, had large windows so that passengers could enjoy the view while dining. As in the *Golden Eagle* triple expansion engines were fitted, with a nominal horsepower of 538.

She was the first paddle steamer in Europe to be fitted for oil-burning. It was the practice of many of the Thames steamers, when coming up the river, to go about below London Bridge and finish the journey in reverse, and the *Crested Eagle* was fitted with a bow rudder to assist this manoeuvre. A hinged mast and telescopic funnel enabled her to pass under the bridge to her berth at Old Swan Pier.

For fifteen years the *Crested Eagle* was one of the most famous paddle steamers on the Thames. When she went into service she joined the already popular *Eagle* and *Golden Eagle* on the Estuary excursions. In 1929 the Company, having sold the *Eagle,* bought as a replacement the ex-Palace steamer *Royal Sovereign,* at a cost of £5,540. The wisdom of this purchase seems questionable, as she was five years older than the ship which she replaced. In fact the *Royal Sovereign* ran for only one season under the G.S.N. flag, although she made 56 trips during that time.

On the sea-going routes the Company had long since abandoned the paddle steamers in favour of screw-driven vessels, and they now began to consider the possibility of using a diesel-powered, screw ship on the Thames. But the advantages of greater deck space and better manoeuvrability that the paddle steamer offered led them to build one more paddler. This new ship was built for them by Messrs. Cammel Laird at Birkenhead, who had built the *Rainbow* in 1837. The ship was launched by Lady Ritchie, wife of Lord Ritchie who was then Chairman of the Port of London Authority. She named the ship *Royal Eagle,* and did so by breaking a bottle of whisky over the bows; this was the first time that whisky had been used to launch a ship. The *Royal Eagle* made her maiden trip three months later. Although ten feet shorter than the *Crested Eagle* her tonnage showed an increase of 400. She could carry 2,000 passengers on her four decks, the upper decks consisting of a glass enclosed saloon, dining saloons to seat 310 people, and a sun-deck above.

And so the 'Navvies' served Londoners until the outbreak of the Second World War. Other ships were added to the fleet during the 30's, the *Isle of Arran* in 1933, the *Laguna Belle* in 1935, and in 1936 the New Medway

Steam Packet Company merged with the G.S.N. But it is the 'Eagle' boats which are best remembered. There had been larger and faster paddle steamers before them, but none were so popular or so well-loved as the *Golden Eagle, Crested Eagle* and *Royal Eagle*.

When the war came all three went into the service of the Royal Navy, the *Golden Eagle* for the second time, but before they did so they carried out one more peace-time task. On September 1st, 2nd and 3rd, 1939, the Thames fleet of the G.S.N. Co. evacuated 19,578 children from London to Felixtowe, Lowestoft and Yarmouth. For the *Crested Eagle* it was the last time that children would crowd on to her broad decks, and the next time she took part in an evacuation she perished on the beaches of Dunkirk.

Chapter Six

THE BIG SINKING

Princess Alice — Collision with the *Bywell Castle* — Great loss of life — New regulations emerge—end of reckless navigation on the Thames.

SEPTEMBER 1878, and Londoners were enjoying the late sunshine of an Indian summer. The Thames excursion season was nearly at an end, but the days were still warm enough to attract hundreds of trippers to a cruise down the river. On the morning of September 3rd, the London Steamboat Company's paddle steamer *Princess Alice* lay at Swan Pier ready to make her daily run to Sheerness. She had been in service on the Thames for twelve years and was one of the most popular steamers on the river. Measuring 219.4ft in length, by 20.2ft in breadth she had two deck saloons with a promenade deck above. The ship had been built at Greenock in 1865 and consecutive owners had made structural changes to increase her carrying capacity. Her hull plates were only 3/16 of an inch thick and the gross tonnage had been increased from the original 171 tons to 250 tons.

The trip down the river was uneventful. There were many children on board, but the ship was not over-crowded.

Scheduled stops were made at Woolwich and Graves-end, where some passengers left the ship and others went on board. At Sheerness there was a further interchange of passengers before the steamer started on her ill-fated return journey. At Gravesend more people joined the ship. Gravesend was at that time popular for its Rosherville Gardens, and many people who had gone there on other boats crowded aboard the *Princess Alice* to return home. The sun was low in the sky as Gravesend was left behind, and a mist began to form over the Kent and Essex marshes. The passengers were in high spirits. A band played on the main fore deck and children danced to the music while their parents sang the popular songs of the day.

On the bridge Captain Grinstead, a man of many years experience, was in command. Behind him John Eyres had just taken the helm from the regular helmsman, an act which was to have a direct effect on the events that followed. Eyres had been a passenger on the downward run. At Gravesend, on the return run, the helmsman, a man named Hopgood, asked if Eyres would take the helm so that he could go ashore. Captain Grinstead was approached and, after being assured that Eyres was a competent seaman, agreed to the change. For a while, Eyres was assisted at the wheel by his brother-in-law. At Erith Reach Eyres was alone at the helm.

As darkness fell the lights of Woolwich could be seen across the flat foreshore of Tripcock Point. Beyond the Point, where the Thames bends sharply, the *Bywell Castle,* an iron-built screw collier, was heading towards the sea. The pilot of the *Bywell Castle* was Christopher Dix, a Trinity House man registered to take vessels down river as far as Gravesend. As the collier approached Tripcock Point, Dix saw the red port light of the *Princess Alice* and assumed that the steamer would shortly cross to the north bank to take advantage of the slacker tide. As the paddle steamer rounded the Point the full force of the tide acted upon her bows and forced her towards the opposite bank.

Eyres was taken completely by surprise, and Grinstead ordered him to hold his starboard helm which should have taken the ship round the Point. But the tide was too strong, the ship continued on its uncontrolled course until it reached slacker water. At that moment she answered to the helm and spun in a half circle; back into the path of the *Bywell Castle*.

The bows of the collier towered twenty feet above the helpless steamer. There was a sudden hush on board as the passengers became aware of the danger. Dix gave orders to stop engines, but it was too late. The knife-like bows plunged deep into the *Princess Alice* just forward of the starboard paddle-box. Within seconds the water was thick with struggling humanity. Some passengers had been thrown from the deck by the impact. Others had jumped for their lives. One man climbed the funnel stays and swung across to the *Bywell Castle*. Ropes were thrown from the bows of the collier, but few people managed to climb them.

Below decks the stairways became jammed as passengers fought to reach the upper deck. Many were drowned as they struggled to escape.

Above the screams and shouts of the panic-stricken crowd the ship's steam whistle echoed across the river as Grinstead heaved on the lanyard. Eyres was still at the wheel and Grinstead called to him to save himself. Seconds later there was a great gush of steam as the boiler fires were extinguished by the rush of water. The weight of the water snapped the ship in two like a broken match.

The stern rose up before plunging to the river bed. The forepart drifted away, and then it too sank. Captain Grinstead stayed with his ship and perished. In four minutes it was all over.

The tragedy had occurred a bare 50 yards from the shore. But few survivors managed to swim to safety. Women in their heavy dresses were dragged down.

Children clung to their mothers, and drowned with them.

A pathetic flotsam of hats, sunshades and children's toys spread slowly across the dark river. In Woolwich the warm evening had brought many people from their houses. The inns and taverns were doing a roaring trade and there was no hint of the disaster that had occurred so close by. The incessant moan of the ship's siren had gone unnoticed. Thamesiders were used to the sounds of the river. It was the cry of a waterman that first attracted attention. As the man brought his boat alongside the pier a small crowd gathered, sensing that something was wrong. Four or five shivering survivors stepped ashore, beneath a tarpaulin in the boat lay four corpses.

As more boats arrived the news of the sinking spread and the search for survivors and victims began. By midnight the offices of the London Steamboat Company were besieged by anxious relatives. By morning the enormity of the disaster became apparent.

It was established that at least 650 people had died, the exact number was never known.

When daylight came the salvaging operations commenced and the foreshore was combed for washed up bodies. Sightseers and sensation-hunters began to flock to the area, making the work more difficult. The search continued for a week and bodies were found on both sides of the river, and as far away as Erith and Limehouse. Four days after the sinking the forepart was raised, to deliver yet more bodies. The news of the raising brought more crowds to the scene and the police had great difficulty in maintaining control. Pickpockets were active and it is probable that a number of bodies were robbed. Many of the victims were recovered by the watermen who probed the river bed with their boathooks, and the tragedy took a sickening turn. The watermen were paid five shillings for each body that they recovered, and fights broke out among them over their grisly catches. The whole grim business turned into a macabre fishing festival, and in fact the horror and shock of the first few days turned into a carnival atmosphere.

Identification was a major problem. Sheds and warehouses were used as temporary mortuaries and anxious relatives trudged from one to another in their pitiful search. There was a sinister incident near Victoria Docks where four bodies were found in a shed. The police had no knowledge of how they got there and they were so badly decomposed that identification was impossible. Their presence remained a mystery, but it is possible that they were the victims of murder.

The Coroner for West Kent was Charles Joseph Carttar. At the age of 69 he was in ailing health and the enormous task so suddenly thrust upon him was to shorten his life. Cartarr was at his home in Greenwich on the evening of September 3rd, when the news was brought to him that there had been a big sinking on the river. The next morning he went to Woolwich and began to organise the search for victims. He was perturbed at the lack of crowd control and the irreverent handling of the bodies. For days he worked with the police, assisting them in their task of arranging a proper identification system and consoling the bereaved.

Gradually the work of collecting and viewing the corpses developed into an efficient routine and by the fifth day only thirty-one bodies remained unidentified. Carttar opened his Inquest on September 6th. After a week's adjournment the Inquest re-opened on September 16th to inquire into the cause of the sinking.

During the following ten weeks over a hundred witnesses were called. Survivors, crew members, shipwrights and eye-witnesses. All gave their accounts of what happened, or what may have happened. The evidence given by the survivors was often moving but of little help. They tended to be lengthy descriptions of personal experiences and much time was wasted in this way. The evidence given by the crew members of both ships was also confusing. Personal loyalties coloured the stories and unfounded accusations were made on both sides. Many witnesses, particularly watermen, spoke of the peculiarity of the tide movement at Tripcock Point. Shipwrights and marine surveyors were called in to give expert opinions on the river-worthiness of the *Princess Alice*.

Generally it was agreed that she was too lightly constructed. An important point considering that collisions were frequent on the river. Key witnesses, of course, were Eyres and Dix. Eyres proved to be quite unreliable, changing his evidence several times. It was established, however, that he had never steered a ship of that length before, and Captain Grinstead's wisdom in letting Eyres take the helm was questioned. Dix was a truculent witness, but he gave his evidence clearly and there was no doubt that he had acted correctly in the situation.

At last, when all the evidence had been heard, the jury retired. Technically they were only required to ascertain the cause of death of one man, a William Beachey whose body was the first to be recovered. The jury were out for fourteen and a half hours, and on November 14th, 1878, they gave their verdict. William Beachey had died from drowning, and blame for the collision was laid equally on the *Princess Alice* and the *Bywell Castle* in that had both ships gone astern when the collision was imminent, then it could have been avoided.

The *Princess Alice* was criticised for not being properly and sufficiently manned, and her life-saving equipment was considered to be inadequate. The most important conclusion was that if proper and stringent rules were laid down for steam navigation on the Thames then all collisions might be avoided in the future.

Before Carttar's Inquest came to an end a Board of Trade enquiry had given its verdict. Heard before Mr.

John Balguy, the Thames magistrate, it lasted from October 14th to November 6th. It took the form of specific charges against Captain Harrison of the *Bywell Castle,* and George Long, First Mate of the *Princess Alice.* The court found that Harrision had acted correctly. Charges that Long had failed to inform Captain Grinstead of the presence of the *Bywell Castle,* were found proven. But the court did not consider that his negligence contributed to the disaster. In the view of the court the *Princess Alice* was to blame for not observing the regulations of the Thames Conservancy Board which state:

'If two vessels under steam are meeting end on, or nearly end on, so as to involve a risk of collision, the helm of both shall be put to port, so that each may pass on the port side of the other'. These rules had been published in 1872, but throughout the inquiry it had become plain that few people had read them, or even knew of their existence. When members of the court visited the scene of the disaster they were appalled to see that vessels on the river passed each other on either side indiscriminately.

On December 11th, 1878, the verdict of yet another court was given. This was the Court of Admiralty set up to hear an action by the London Steamboat Company against the owners of the *Bywell Castle*. The court found that both parties were to blame. The *Princess Alice,* they said, was navigated in a careless and reckless manner. The *Bywell Castle* was also at fault in going hard to port before the moment of impact. The case went to a Court of Appeal. They upheld the view that the *Princess Alice* was at fault, but maintained that although the *Bywell Castle*'s last-minute manoeuvre was wrong it was not the cause of the accident.

Undoubtedly the key figures in the tragedy were Captain Grinstead and John Eyres. Grinstead had been described as 'a careful, nice man who understood his business thoroughly'. Allowing Eyres to take the helm was a fatal lapse of that carefulness. It would not be true to say that Eyres acted recklessly or irresponsibly. He was unfamiliar with the ship, and was not aware of the peculiarity of the cross-current at Tripcock Point. His inexperience led to the greatest tragedy ever to occur in British inland waters, either before or since.

By the end of the year the incident had been forgotten by the general public. After the inquest Charles Carttar returned to his home in Greenwich. Two years later he died of a heart disease that had been accelerated by his devotion to duty. In December, Her Royal Highness Princess Alice, died of diphtheria at the age of 35. Her death was mourned by the nation, but death from such diseases as diphtheria, influenza and pneumonia were common. The loss of the ship that bore the royal name had brought death on a scale unknown in Britain.

But those who lived by and worked on the river did not forget. New rules for river navigation were recommended by the Board of Trade. They required that all vessels should keep to the starboard side of the river, and that any vessel crossing the river, or turning, should not obstruct other river traffic. Strict rules for life-saving equipment were drawn up, and it became obligatory to carry lifejackets for every person on board.

The rules were applied with typical Victorian thoroughness. For over sixty years steamships, sail and other types of craft had used London's river as a giant dodgem track. Now, at last, commonsense prevailed and the Thames became an orderly waterway befitting the greatest city in the world.

Chapter Seven

FREAKS AND FAILURES

Unorthodox designs — Twin hulls — Bessemer's swinging saloon —
Some novel forms of propulsion.

In the early days of the steamboat many strange and
elaborate craft were designed. Some engineers, like John
Fitch, tried to harness the new power to already proven
methods of propulsion, such as the oar or paddle. The
stern paddle-wheel was popular for many years, particularly on the American and Australian riverboats, but
by the middle of the nineteenth century the twin,
side mounted paddle-wheel had become the generally
accepted formula, and marine engineers concentrated on
the design of more powerful engines and better hulls.
There were others, however, who continued to experiment with unorthodox methods. Some designs failed
because they were based on false engineering principles.
Others worked, but were either too costly to run or left no
room for further development. These vessels are now
looked upon as freaks, but they were genuine attempts to
find a better alternative to the accepted principle.

We have already seen that Brunel's refusal to accept a
commonly-held theory led to the design of the first ocean
steamship. Without experiment there can be no development, and these 'freak' ships have a place in the story of
the paddle steamer.

The advantage of twin hulls attracted the attention of several designers, and one of the earliest vessels so de-singed was the first steam warship, the *Demologos*. She was built in 1814 at New York to the plans of Robert Fulton. Her purpose was to act as a coastal defence vessel, and to break the British blockade. The hulls were made of wood and were placed 15ft apart. The 16ft diameter paddle-wheel was fitted between the hulls, where it would be protected from shot. One hull contained the engine, while the other contained the copper boilers. The armament consisted of twenty 32 pounders which fired red-hot cannonballs.

On 4th July, 1815, the *Demologos* steamed over a distance of 53 miles at an average speed of 6.3 m.p.h. Two months later, fully laden with stores and ammunition, she made another trip at an average speed of 5.5 m.p.h.

The ship never saw action and after the war she was laid up at New York. On 4th June, 1829, she was destroyed by an explosion on board.

When she was built exaggerated accounts of her size appeared in some British newspapers. One Scottish paper gave her dimensions as 300ft long and 200ft broad. In fact, her length was a mere 156ft with a breadth of 56ft.

The twin hull idea was also used on the Thames paddle steamer, the *Gemini*, in 1850. She had iron hulls 157.6ft in length, each hull being 8.5ft wide and separated by a gap of 9.6ft. Accommodation was for 800 to 1,000 passengers. Her inventor, Mr. Peter Borrie, anticipated that there would be a large demand for river services during the 1851 Exhibition and it was hoped that the *Gemini* would outclass all the steamboats that were operating on the river at that time. Unfortunately the ship did not live up to her designer's expectations. When she made her trial trip, the single, central mounted paddle-wheel strove hard to propel the vessel, but her speed was practically nil, and against the tide she made no headway at all.

In 1857 a double-hulled steamer, the *Alliance,* went into service on the Clyde. She was 140ft long by 30ft beam and seems to have been more successful than the *Gemini.* She had the distinction of being the first Clyde steamer with a main deck saloon.

The English Channel service saw several freak ships, and all were built with one purpose in mind. The notoriously rough crossing was feared by many would-be visitors to France, and a ship that would provide a smooth crossing in any weather would obviously attract many passengers.

Captain Dicey, formerly of the Indian Navy, had seen catamarans in eastern waters and had been impressed by their stability. In 1874 he designed the *Castalia,* a double-hulled iron vessel of 1,533 tons. The ship was built by Thames Ironworks, the hulls were 290ft long with a beam of 20ft and the arched girders that joined them were of immense strength.

The distance between the hulls was 26ft, and two paddle-wheels in tandem operated in this space. They were driven by two, direct acting diagonal engines placed one in each hull. Rudders were fitted fore and aft and the controls were duplicated so that the ship could travel forward or reverse equally well, thus speeding up the turn-around time in port.

The twin hulls produced the desired effect, but she was deplorably slow. After only two seasons she was taken out of service and became part of an isolation hospital at Dartford. She was broken up in Holland in 1907.

Sir Henry Bessemer was a famous 19th century engineer. He invented the process of converting iron into steel by forcing air through molten metal. He was also a very poor sailor. Sir Henry's business took him on frequent trips to France, and every trip was a nightmare, so he

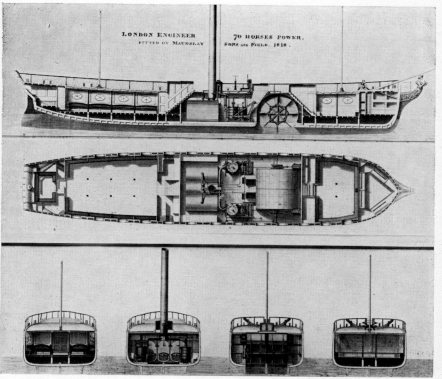

Fig. 11 — Drawings of the LONDON ENGINEER. A freak ship that
sailed on the Thames. Built in 1818. (Photo Science Museum, London).

Fig. 12 — Triple expansion engines of the CALEDONIA, 1934.
(Photo Bass Charrington Ltd.).

decided to design a ship with a saloon that would not roll.

In the grounds of his mansion in Denmark Hill he built a 20ft model of a cabin which was mounted on a central pivot and was kept level by a suspended pendulum. The idea seemed to work, and in 1869 Sir Henry floated the Bessemer Saloon Ship Company. With his reputation it was not difficult to find backers and the company started with a capital of £250,000.

The ship was built at Hull by the Earle Company. She was 349ft long by 40ft wide and had a gross tonnage of 1,974. Two pairs of paddle-wheels were provided with the object of giving the ship a speed of 20 knots. Bessemer's brainchild, the saloon, was 70ft long, 35ft wide, 20ft high and weighed 130 tons. The idea was that the saloon would swing freely and be independent of the movements of the hull.

On May 8th, 1875, Sir Henry sailed in the *Bessemer* for Calais with a party of invited guests. The day was hardly the best for proving his design, for the sea was like glass.

What was apparent, however, was that the two paddles on each side were set too close together, so that the rear paddle-wheels were trying to work in water that was already moving at high speed when it reached them. The effect was to produce a drag that held the ship's speed down to a mere 11 knots. In addition she was slow to answer to the helm, and on arrival at Calais three attempts were made to enter the harbour. The third attempt resulted in a violent collision with the pier, whereupon the French authorities arrested the ship until a payment of £2,500 for damages was agreed upon. On the return trip to Dover the experience was repeated, and Dover pier also sustained heavy damage.

The next voyage was made in rough weather, but passengers complained that the motion of the saloon was worse than in any other part of the ship. Sir Henry then came up with the idea of a hydraulic brake. This was controlled by a man who kept watch on a spirit level, and whenever the saloon moved from the level he would try to correct the sway with the brake.

This made matters even worse, for while the ship moved in one direction the saloon moved in the other. Finally the saloon was locked in position, but the problems of speed and manoeuvrability still remained, and when Dover pier was rammed for the second time, Sir Henry gave up.

The ship was sold for scrap, but the saloon was preserved. For many years it stood in the grounds of the Horticultural College at Hextable in Kent. It was destroyed by a direct hit during a bombing raid in the Second World War.

In 1887 another double-hulled steamer was built for the cross-channel service. Built on the same principle as the *Castalia,* the *Express* had a gross tonnage of 1,924 and engines of 3,600 I.H.P. She was built by Leslies of Hebburn for the Channel Steamship Company, but was taken over by the builders when the Company went into liquidation. Her two hulls were each 302ft in length by 183ft beam, and two paddle-wheels were placed between the hulls. The steering gear was steam-operated and gave constant trouble.

She was faster than the *Castalia,* reaching a maximum speed of 14 knots, and in rough weather rolled only about five degrees, although she pitched heavily. The builders renamed her *Calais-Douvres,* and when she went into service she completed her maiden voyage in ninety-seven minutes. She was later bought by the London, Chatham and Dover Railway Company, sold to France in 1880, and laid up as a hulk in 1887. In 1889 she was broken up on the Thames.

Apart from double-hulls and double-paddles there were also a number of unusual experiments in the form of propulsion. A Scots engineer, John Kibble, designed and had built the *Queen of Beauty*. This ship was 137.8ft long and had drive shafts fitted fore and aft, each shaft carrying a drum. Between the drums ran a continuous belt fitted with paddle-floats. Despite the fact that the engine was provided by the famous Robert Napier, this waterborne tractor was not a success.

Similar to Kibble's vessel was the *Ocean Palace,* the invention of an Australian named Wilcox.

This vessel also employed the double-hull principle.

An even more unusual idea was the roller ship. After twelve years of experiments Robert Fryer built, in the early 'eighties, the *Alice*. The triangular deck rested on three huge wheels which supplied the buoyancy. A series of buckets around the wheels acted as paddle-floats and were intended to propel the vessel when driven by the steam engines on deck. It was also intended that the vessel should be amphibious. The whole idea failed in practice.

One very novel design that apparently had some success was the Thames steamer, the *Propellor*. Built at Blackwall by Ditchburn and Mare for the Blackwall Railway Company, she was designed especially for the river trade. The paddles consisted of single iron blades which dipped into the water and then moved back in grasshopper fashion. The 30 n.h.p. engine drove the ship at about 10 knots and no wash was created, thus avoiding damage to other vessels.

The exact date of the construction of the *Propellor* is not known, but she is believed to have operated on the Blackwall to Gravesend service sometime between 1840 and 1845.

Another famous Thames steamer was the *London Engineer*. Internal, double paddle-wheels were the unique feature of this vessel. She was built in 1818 for the Margate service by Brent of Rotherhithe. The bell-crank engine, by Maudslay, drove the two paddle-wheels at a rate of 28 revolutions per minute. As the wheels were totally enclosed the stream of water to them was kept constant by air forced into the waterway by two pumps. The steamer was quite large for her day, 120ft long by 24ft in beam, and was fitted with a comfortable saloon. But her design was not a success and she had a very short life.

Some of the ideas put forward by these early pioneers may seem ludicrous today, and it is easy to laugh at the misfortunes of the *Bessemer,* or at the non-progress of the *Gemini.* But these were men's dreams and large fortunes were sometimes lost in the rude awakening.

The *Alice* cost £14,000 to develop. Sir Henry Bessemer contributed £41,000 to his ship. More inventors have died penniless than have become rich and famous, and the history of the paddle steamer had its share of men who staked all and lost.

Chapter Eight

THE GREAT LEVIATHAN

Brunel returns to ship designing — Eastern Steam Navigation
Company — The *Great Eastern* is built — Problems of launching —
Explosion on board — Brunel dies — Atlantic failure—cable-
laying—success at last.

MANY of the freak ships were built by men who had little
knowledge of marine engineering, but the largest and
most costly of them all was designed by the greatest
engineer of his day. Isambard Kingdom Brunel.

After designing the *Great Western* and the *Great
Britain,* Brunel returned to his main work of constructing
railways. But in the 1840's he became disillusioned; the
tremendous boom that followed the success of the first
railways led to wild speculation, and Brunel found that
his designs were being dictated by commercial considerations. No longer was he able to indulge his forward-looking
ideas, and what had once been a great adventure became
drudgery. The intense rivalry between the many railway
companies that were springing up all over the country
sickened him, and he began to look again towards the
sea, where there was still scope for new and revolutionary
development.

The discovery of gold in Australia had led to an
immigration boom to that country and the shipping
companies were beginning to turn their attention towards
the long haul to the Southern Hemisphere.

No ship afloat was capable of steaming to Australia

without stopping for coal at the Cape of Good Hope, which meant that bunker coal had to be shipped from Penarth to the Cape.

Brunel began to toy with the idea of a ship large enough to carry its own coal there and back. The vessel would be six times larger than anything ever built before, and it seemed unlikely that such a big step forward would be acceptable to any steamship company. There was one, however, that was prepared to listen to Brunel's plan.

The Eastern Steam Navigation Company had been formed in 1851 to trade with India, Australia and the Far East. They had suffered a staggering blow when the British Government awarded the eastern mail contract to P & O and were keen to adopt any scheme that would enable them to beat their rivals. Brunel's idea was greeted with enthusiasm. In July 1852, the Company appointed him as their Engineer, and invited tenders for the construction of the hull and engines.

The dimensions of the *Leviathan,* as the ship was originally called, were 692ft long 82ft in beam. This unprecedented length created special problems for a ship that would have to encounter heavy seas. There was a danger that she would break her back when the bow and stern were supported by only two waves, or when poised admidships by a single wave. As he had done in the design of the *Great Britain,* Brunel applied his bridge-building technique to the hull. It was built in the form of a huge girder, with a double skin and frame. The deck was also double and was cellular in form. The plates of the inner and outer hull were $\frac{3}{4}$ inch thick and were secured to the frames by 4 inch x 4 inch angle irons. Watertight compartments were provided by transverse bulkheads placed 60 ft apart and there were no openings in the bulkheads below the second deck. Two longtitudinal bulkheads, placed 36ft apart, extended for 350ft of the ship's length.

The decision to use both paddle and screw propulsion was the result of two considerations. First, at that time, it would not have been possible to use a single paddleshaft or screwshaft capable of delivering sufficient horsepower to propel a ship of that size. Second, it was the intention of the owners to take the ship into shallow waters, which also dictated the draught of the ship. The screw was designed to be 25ft in diameter which meant that at times a large area of the screw would be out of the water. The paddle-wheels would then compensate for the subsequent loss of power. The power ratio of the screw to paddles was approximately two to one, and the paddle-wheels were 60ft in diameter.

Brunel's specification for the engines required an output of 4,000 i.h.p. from the screw engines and 2,600 i.h.p. from the paddle engines, both working at 15lb steam pressure. When the engines were built they actually worked at 25lb pressure, giving a total of nearly 10,000 i.h.p. The screw engines were built by James Watt and Company at Birmingham and the paddle engines by John Scott Russell and Company.

Russell was a famous ship designer and builder, and it was at his yard in Millwall that the ship was built. The Thames at that point was too narrow to permit a lengthways launching so the hull was built broadside on to the river.

The paddle-engines were built in a yard adjacent to the ship and although larger than any engines built before, they weighed 836 tons, were orthodox in design. They were of the oscillating type with four cylinders each 74 inches in diameter with a stroke of 14ft. The screw engines were more original and were the result of long discussions between Brunel and James Watt and Company. There were four cylinders, 7ft in diameter with a 4ft stroke, arranged in pairs on opposite sides of the crankshaft. They worked directly onto the shaft which had two cranks set at 45°. The complete unit weighed 500 tons and the 36-ton, cast-iron propellor was carried on a shaft 150ft in length and weighing 60 tons.

Steam for the paddle-engines was provided from four boilers, each weighing 50 tons and containing 40 tons of water. The screw engines had six boilers of 55 tons each and contained 45 tons of water. The ten boilers were served by five funnels, and, as a precaution against failure of both screw and paddles, six masts carried a spread of 6,500 yards of sail.

To launch the giant hull Brunel had designed a set of roller cradles which could also be used for lifting the ship from the water when she was in need of repair or examination. But as work progressed the costs mounted. Scott Russell ran into serious financial difficulties and more money had to be poured into the project. By the time the ship was ready to be launched nearly £300,000 had been paid by the Eastern Steam Navigation Company. Economies had to be made, and Brunel's launching cradle was abandoned in favour of a cheaper method.

When at last the day of the launch arrived, Brunel insisted that only a few people should be present. He would be in command of the operation and it was essential that all those concerned should be able to hear his orders. On November 3rd, 1858, Brunel made his way to Millwall for what he hoped would be the greatest moment in his life. What he found there filled him with alarm. The E.S.N. Co., intent on recovering some of their losses, had sold 3,000 tickets for the ceremony. The shipyard was swarming with people in festive mood who had come to see the great spectacle. At twelve-thirty Brunel mounted the platform to direct the operation.

The hull was supported in two cradles, placed fore and aft. To control its movement each cradle was held by chains to checking drums. When the wedges holding the cradles were removed, the hull refused to budge and

Fig. 13 — P.S. GLEN SANNOX, the Glasgow and South Western Railway steamer. (Photo Glasgow Museums and Art Galleries).

Fig. 14 — P.S. IVANHOE. The 'teetotal' ship.
(Photo Glasgow Museums and Art Galleries).

Fig. 15 — The Southampton Co.'s P.S. BOURNEMOUTH QUEEN.
Ran excursions to the South Coast resorts and Isle of Wight).
(Photo courtesy Red Funnel Steamers).

Fig. 16 — The PRINCESS ELIZABETH in Weymouth Bay.
(Photo by R. Bruce Grice, courtesy of "Ships Monthly").

Brunel called for the use of hydraulic rams.

Under the pressure of the rams the bow suddenly moved a distance of three feet, the crew manning the drum on the stern cradle were so distracted by the crowd that they were not aware of what was happening. Suddenly the stern commenced to move, snatching at the checking drum, and the mutilated body of a man who had been standing on the winch handle was hurled into the air.

The ceremony was abandoned and during the following weeks, several attempts were made to get the ship into the water. Brunel designed new hydraulic presses and gradually the 12,000 ton hull was pushed down the slipways. Finally, on January 31st, 1858, the last great effort was made and the *Leviathan,* or *Great Eastern* as she was now officially called, slid gently into the water.

The final cost of the delayed launch had been too much for the already impoverished Eastern Steam Navigation Company. They went into liquidation and the *Great Eastern* was taken over by a new concern, the Great Ship Company.

Further delays occurred before the ship was ready for its sea trials, and it was on September 5th, 1858, that Brunel boarded his ship to supervise the trials. But it was not to be, the engineer had only been on board a few hours when he was seized by a stroke. The months of anxiety, sleepless nights and overwork had reduced him to a very sick man. He was taken to his home in Duke Street where he lay waiting for the news of the trial. Completely paralysed, his mind was still alert and all he wished for before he died was the news that his greatest venture was a success.

On September 7th the ship set sail for Weymouth. On board were reporters, privileged passengers and representatives of the engine manufacturers. After working the ship up to 13 knots Captain Harrison, who was in command, brought her round the Kent coast and to within sight of Hastings.

Most of the passengers were in the dining saloon and a few had gathered in the bows when there was a tremendous explosion. The forward funnel was ripped from the deck by the force and the main saloon was completely demolished. A steam pipe from the paddle engine room had burst, five of the crew died and it was only the immense strength of the ship that prevented the disaster from being far worse. It seems that Brunel's designs were fated to prove themselves in spectacular and unexpected fashion.

For the great engineer this was the final cruel stroke, and in the evening of September 15th he died.

The *Great Eastern* made her first Atlantic crossing in June 1860, for her new owners felt that this service would be more profitable than the Australian route. In fact she was never a success on this run. She could accommodate 800 first class, 2,000 second class and 1,200 third class passengers, but two more disasters brought financial ruin to her owners.

In September 1861, the *Great Eastern* met heavy weather when only three days out from Liverpool. One of her lifeboats became detached and was in danger of fouling the paddle wheel. When the captain put the ship astern so that the boat could be cut away, the rudder-post snapped and the ship turned side on to the pounding seas. In a short time the paddle wheels were torn from their hubs and before the crew could repair the rudder, considerable damage had been done to the saloons.

The following summer the ship hit an uncharted reef outside New York harbour. Examination of the hull revealed that a hole 85ft long by 5ft wide had been torn in the outer skin. The inner skin was untouched and, once again, the soundness of Brunel's design had been proved.

These two accidents cost £13,000 in repairs and after

one more trip the *Great Eastern* was put up for sale. She was bought by three former shareholders of the old company, and they immediately chartered the ship to the Telegraph Construction Company for cable-laying.

So, at last, the *Great Eastern* embarked on a new career that was to be entirely successful. In July 1865, she left Ireland to lay a new cable across the Atlantic. After 1,200 miles the cable snapped and all efforts to retrieve it failed. The following year she set out again, this time to succeed. On her return voyage attempts were made to recover the cable that had been lost the previous year. After several tries it was found and grappled, a new cable was spliced on and the transatlantic cable was completed.

Having proved herself in her new role, the *Great Eastern* went on to lay cables from France to America, Bombay to Aden and along the Red Sea. The Great Eastern Steamship Company, as the owners now called themselves, prospered and when her cable laying activities were over, they refitted the ship for passenger service. But she was never a success in this kind of activity and at one time was used as a floating fair and exhibition on the River Mersey.

In 1888 she was broken up on Merseyside. Legend has it that when the double hull was cut open the skeleton of a man was found in one of the compartments. The probability of such a story seems highly suspect; but to the gullible it explained her many misfortunes.

The *Great Eastern* was a vessel born out of her time, created by a man whose genius put him in the forefront of his contemporaries. She was a giant, some would say a monster, yet in her construction lessons were learned that made possible the building of the great ocean liners of today. Even so, it was many years before any ship exceeding her dimensions was built.

Chapter Nine

THE POWER AND THE GLORY

The development of paddle engines — The atmospheric engine — side-lever — direct-acting — steeple engines — oscillating engines — boilers — compound engines — triple-expansion — types of paddle-wheels.

THE application of the steam engine to ship propulsion created many difficulties for the early pioneers. Before marine engines were designed, attempts were made to adapt the primitive engines which were in use at that time for other purposes. Thomas Newcomen's engine, designed in 1710 was originally intended for pumping water from the mines in Cornwall. It had two major disadvantages; first the steam was condensed in the cylinder, which entailed an enormous waste of heat, second its motion was vertical, which was adequate for operating a single pump but lacked the power to drive a ship through the water.

This type of engine was known as 'Atmospheric'. A weight pulled up a piston inside an iron cylinder, steam was injected into the cylinder and was then condensed by a jet of cold water. The piston was then forced down by atmospheric pressure and could be made to do useful work through a series of rods and levers.

In 1765 James Watt improved upon Newcomen's principle by the invention of a separate condenser, and although the vertical movement was retained, his engine was powerful enough to propel a boat. In 1774 Watt joined with Matthew Boulton to form the company of Boulton and Watt, and it was one of their engines that powered Fulton's *Clermont*.

William Symington's engine also worked on the atmospheric principle, but in the *Charlotte Dundas* he used a separate condenser, which was considered to be an infringement of Watt's patent.

The early marine engines had their cylinders placed vertically as was the practice on land. The pistons were connected to a pivoted beam which actuated the flywheel shaft. On stationary engines the beam was placed above the cylinder, but in the marine engine the practice was to place the beam below the cylinder in order to keep the centre of gravity low.

Beam engines, however, were used for many years on some American steamers, and were based on the design, perfected in 1822, by Robert L. Stevenson. They had a single, vertical cylinder, working at about 65 p.s.i., placed between the legs of a double A frame, the apex of which carried the beam. The paddle-wheels were always of a large diameter, at least 20ft, and the tall paddle-boxes, extending upwards to the top deck, were a distinctive feature of these vessels.

Most of the credit for the development of the side lever engine must go to Robert Napier. His first engine of this type was built in 1824 and was fitted in the paddle steamer *Leven*. The engine had a single cylinder and it was found that with this arrangement the engine could be started with the piston at either end of its stroke.

Napier's engines generally had two cylinders of 5ft diameter and 2ft stroke. The steam pressure was about 15lb per square inch and the engine developed appproximately 700 h.p. Condensers were of the type whereby the incoming steam was met by a jet of cold water.

Another interesting side-lever engine was that fitted to the *Ruby* in 1836. The *Ruby* was built for service on the

Thames and her engines were built by Seaward and Co. They consisted of two cyclinders 3ft 4 inches in diameter by 3ft 6 inches stroke. In common with most side-lever engines they were efficient but excessively heavy and required considerable space. In addition to the 18ft length the boilers took up 24ft, so that 42ft of the ship's length of 155ft were occupied by machinery.

Various attempts were made to reduce the space required by side-lever engines. In some designs the cylinders were placed fore and aft instead of athwartships.

One cylinder was placed fore or aft of the crankshaft, which drove it through side levers, while the other was set underneath the shaft, the piston driving the crank by side rods.

This was followed by the direct-acting engine in which both cylinders were placed under the crankshaft. The first set of engines of this type were installed in H.M.S. *Gorgon,* and were built by Seaward and Co. In addition to the saving in space they weighed 60 tons less than side-lever engines of the same power. The two cylinders were 9ft 4 inches in diameter with a stroke of 5ft 6 inches. The overhead crankshaft was supported by eight, 7 inch diameter columns. The piston rods were guided by a parallel motion, from which the pumps were also driven, and one objection to the design was that the short connecting rods imposed a heavy strain on this mechanism. In 1839 Seaward and Capel introduced an engine with open-topped cylinders to overcome this problem.

The absence of top covers on the cylinders allowed long connecting rods to be attached to the pistons. Steam was supplied at 8lb per square inch, but the absence of the top covers meant that steam could only be applied to one side of the piston, the working stroke being obtained by atmospheric pressure on the piston top.

A set of engines built to this design were installed in the iron paddle steamer *Sapphire* in 1842 and were satisfactory in service. Similar engines were also used in the cross-channel steamers *Alliance* and *Havre* in 1856.

The 'steeple' engine was another space-saving design and got its name from the piston rod guides which projected above the engine in steeple fashion. They were introduced in 1837 by G. Forrester and Co. of Liverpool, who installed one in the *Rainbow*. In 1839, Joseph Maudslay and Joshua Field patented a 'return connecting rod' device in their steeple engine. The piston had two rods attached at the upper ends to a crosshead, with a connecting rod working downward onto the crank.

This design was improved upon in 1842 by David Napier of Millwall who used four piston rods, two on either side of the crankshaft. Napier further improved the design by reverting to two rods which passed through the top cover of the cylinder and extended upwards on either side of the crankshaft. Above the shaft the rods were linked by a crosshead working in cylindrical guides. The connecting rod worked downwards from the crosshead onto the crankshaft. Slide valves of the locomotive type controlled the steam distribution. The East India Company used several of these engines in their river steamers.

The 'return piston rod' was another device used to permit the use of a long connecting rod. In this type of engine the single piston rod was connected to a four-armed crosshead. Four rods passed downwards from the crosshead to a pair of crosspieces, and a forked connecting rod drove upwards to the crankshaft.

Maudslay and Field patented their steeple engine in 1839 and in 1844 they patented another design, the 'siamese' engine. The double cylinders of this engine were placed fore and aft under the paddle-shaft. Two piston rods were attached to a double T-shaped crosshead, the tail of which moved in guides between the cylinders. The connecting rod was also attached to the crosshead tail and worked upwards onto the crankshaft.

Of all the various types and designs of paddle steamer engines the side-lever and steeple were the most popular during the early part of the 19th century. Direct-acting engines found some favour, particularly in warships where the cylinders were placed horizontally so as to keep the machinery below the water line. Diagonal engines, in which the cylinders were fixed on an inclined bed, were also used in many paddle steamers.

Perhaps the most interesting of all paddle steamer engines was the oscillating engine, in which the cylinders were mounted in trunnions, allowing them to follow the motion of the crankshaft.

The piston rod acted directly onto the crankshaft without the use of connecting-rods, crossheads or guides. The use of oscillating cylinders had been proposed as early as 1785 by Murdoch, who was assistant to James Watt. In 1822 the *Aaron Manby* was fitted with oscillating engines of 80 h.p. Joseph Maudslay patented an engine of this type in 1827. The engine had two cylinders placed below the crankshaft. The central trunnions connected the exhaust side of the cylinders to the condenser, which was placed between the cylinders, and the steam supply was delivered through the outer trunnions. D-shaped valves were contained in a valve chest at the exhaust side of the cylinders and the steam inlet connected to the valve chests via circular passages in the cylinder wall. The valves were driven by eccentrics on the paddle-shaft. The Thames steamer *Endeavour* was fitted with 20 h.p. engines of this type by Maudslay and plied between London and Richmond from 1829 to 1840.

John Penn of Greenwich made substantial improve-ments to this design by placing the valve chests on the cylinder sides between the trunnions, thus producing a more compact engine. He also achieved considerable weight reduction by the use of wrought iron in place of cast iron in the construction of the framework.

Scott Russell, of *Great Eastern* fame, designed a three cylinder oscillating engine in 1853. One cylinder was placed vertically and the others at 60° to it. The advantage of this arrangement was that it gave an even turning motion to the crankshaft. The Egyptian Government's yacht *Cleopatra* employed a set of these engines which were of 882 h.p.

The oscillating engine was slow to achieve popularity with marine engineers. Their movement in the confined area of a ship's engine-room was considered to be dangerous, and in those days there were already enough dangers to contend with.

But their efficiency could not be ignored and engines of this type were built to huge dimensions, notably in the *Great Eastern*. The *Pacific,* an iron ship of 1,469 tons, was built by Scott Russell in 1853 and had engines of 1,684 h.p. The oscillating cylinders measured 6ft 2 inches in diameter by 7ft stroke and drove 27ft diameter paddle-wheels. In 1860, an iron paddle steamer, the *Leinster,* was fitted with oscillating engines which represented a high peak in the development of marine engines. Producing 4,751 i.h.p. they had two cylinders, each measuring 8ft 2 inches by 6ft 6 inches in stroke, placed below the crankshaft. Both cylinders had two valve chests arranged on opposite sides of the trunnions, so that the irrespective weights were balanced. To ensure that the valve motion worked independently of the cylinder's oscillation a sliding rod, driven by an eccentric, had a curved slot at its lower end accommodating two slide-blocks connected to the valve rods. The condenser was placed between the cylinders and contained the two air pumps which were driven by an intermediate crank on the paddle shaft.

The feed and bilge pumps were driven by brackets attached to the cylinders.

The *Leinster* was 343ft long and 35ft in beam with a displacement of 2,000 tons. On her trials she achieved

$17\frac{3}{4}$ knots with her engines turning at $25\frac{1}{2}$ revolutions per minute on a steam pressure of 20 pounds per square inch.

The paddle engines already described worked on relatively low steam pressures. The governing factor in steam pressure is, of course, the boiler and even at low pressure explosions were frequent. The use of low pressure necessitated large cylinders, which created difficulties in accommodating them within a ship's hull.

The boilers for atmospheric engines were very simple. They were barely strong enough to carry the weight of water contained within them, and were externally fired. The flues were brick-built, and sometimes a brick funnel was used.

Internal furnace flues came into use from about 1820. The boiler was box-shaped, the rectangular flues were built into the boiler and were completely surrounded by water. The substitution of tubes for the rectangular flues marked an important step forward in boiler design. Fire tubes had been used in locomotives from the time of Stephenson's 'Rocket', and their use in marine boilers was pioneered by Thomas Cochrane, tenth Earl of Dundonald. Tubed boilers had an internal furnace with a combustion chamber from which the furnace gases passed through the tubes in the water space to a smoke box, and thence to the funnel.

Box boilers of this type were in common use in the Royal Navy after 1850, and the steam pressure was usually about 25 p.s.i.

As the demand for higher steam pressures grew it became necessary to abandon the box boiler in favour of a cylindrical pattern. The changeover was not immediate and between 1862 and 1868 a number of boilers were patented which contained features common to both types.

Eventually, however, the cylindrical boiler became universally used, the most famous being that known as the 'Scotch' type. The working pressure of the Scotch boiler when it was introduced in 1870, was about 60 p.s.i. By 1890 pressures of up to 135 p.s.i. were obtained. The corrugated flue, invented in 1877 by Fox, was an important factor in the design of these boilers. It was able to stand up to much higher external pressures than the tubular or rectangular type, and also gave a greater heating surface. Water-tube boilers, in which the water passes through tubes and is heated externally, superseded the Scotch boiler. Nevertheless their origin goes back as far as 1766, when William Blakey patented a boiler with inclined water-tubes. John Penn also used water-tube boilers in 1842 in his Thames paddle steamers.

One of the reasons for using low pressures was that in the early days condensers were not efficient enough to allow vessels to travel very far without replenishing their boilers. In the river steamers this was no problem, they had unlimited fresh water supplies around them.

Sea-going vessels, however, had to carry fresh-water supplies, or use sea water. The use of sea water resulted in salt deposits on the heating surfaces, and the boilers had to be 'blown out' periodically. Blow out cocks were opened every hour or so and steam forced out the heavily salted water. Condensers consisted of a tank in which the exhausted steam met a jet of sea water and the resulting mixture of condensed steam and sea water was pumped back to the boiler.

The surface condenser eliminated these problems and its introduction paved the way for high pressure engines in sea-going vessels. In this type of condenser the cooling sea water was pumped through tubes and the steam condensed on the outer surface of the tubes. James Watt and David Napier both invented surface condensers, but Samuel Hall's patent of 1831 was the first practical application of this method. In Hall's condenser the cooling water was pumped through a tank and the exhaust steam was carried in copper tubes.

87

The paddle steamer *Wilberforce* was fitted with Hall's condensers in 1837 and ran between London and Hull until 1841, when the tubes were found to be coated with mud. The condensers were replaced by the jet type and for some years this unfortunate experience served as a setback to Hall's invention.

Later the surface condenser became generally adopted, and apart from its original function of keeping the boilers clean, helped in the development of engines operating on high steam pressures.

The thermal efficiency of a steam engine, where steam is used in only one cylinder, suffers because of the heat losses due to the alternate heating and cooling of the cylinder walls. This can be overcome by using steam at high pressure in one cylinder, and then at low pressure in a second cylinder. This is known as compounding, and if a third cylinder is added the method is known as 'triple-expansion'. Compound engines were used in paddle steamers on the Rhine in 1830 and on the Thames in 1846.

The Halfpenny Fare Steamers, *Ant, Bee, Cricket* and *Fly* had high pressure engines. The *Cricket* was soon replaced by the *New Cricket,* and in August 1847 the boiler of this vessel exploded. It was during a busy part of the day while the boat was waiting near London Bridge. Seventeen people were killed and sixty severely injured. The fault, however, was not with the pressure system. The ship's engineer had screwed down the safety valves in order to get more speed from his engines, and then went off duty without telling his relief of his stupid action.

Despite this unfortunate accident the compound engine eventually came into use on many paddle steamers. The arrangement of the cylinders took various forms, diagonal, horizontal, each builder had his own preference, but compound diagonal eventually became the most popular.

Triple expansion was used on many of the larger

steamers, such as the *Crested Eagle, Royal Eagle* and *Majestic,* and was the ultimate in paddle steamer engine development.

The steam turbine was developed for screw driven vessels. The diesel engine was used on some paddlers, particularly the paddle tugs of the Royal Navy, and a diesel-electric packet, the *Talisman,* ran on the Clyde for several years.

Once the steam engine had been successfully adapted for marine use it was not long before engineers began to consider ways of improving the paddle-wheel. The early wheels were simply a series of radius arms with flat, wooden floats fixed in the axial plane at their outer ends. Consequently each float produced a heavy shock as it entered the water, with a resulting strain on the arm, and did not become fully effective until it was nearly at the bottom of its cycle. This strain and loss of efficiency was repeated as the float moved upwards against the water above it.

In 1833 Joshua Field invented a cycloidal wheel, but abandoned the idea.

It was re-invented in 1835 by Elijah Galloway. Each float consisted of four separate wrought-iron blades set stepwise in advance of one another towards the circumference, and approximately in a cycloidal curve. The width of the blades decreased, the inner blades being wider than the outer, and the radial arms were set slightly off the true radius. This arrangement considerably lessened the shock on entering the water, while the escape of air and water between the blades was facilitated. Galloway's wheel was first tried out on City of Dublin packet steamers, and the *Great Western* was fitted with paddle-wheels of this type.

A problem experienced in ocean-going paddle steamers was the change of immersion depth of the floats that resulted from the consumption of coal on board, for as the

89

ship got lighter so the floats dipped less deeply into the water.

A reefing paddle-wheel was introduced in 1843 by Brunet as a means of correcting this. The floats were arranged so that they could be moved simultaneously along the arms from the centre by the turn of a winch handle on the deck.

Variations in the shape of floats were tried, a successful example being John Rennie's diamond-shape of 1839. The floats entered the water pointed end first and so reduced the suddeness of the shock. The Thames steamer *Lily* was converted to this design in 1840, with a resulting 14% increase in speed.

All of these designs went a long way towards improving the efficiency of the paddle-wheel, but maximum thrust could only be obtained if the floats entered the water vertically, or nearly so, and remained vertical throughout their period of immersion. John Fitch realised this when he used his canoe-type paddles in 1786, and the Thames steamer *Propellor* employed a single blade moving vertically through the water.

A feathering float, that is a float which changes its angle as it revolves with the wheel, was patented by Robertson Buchanan of Glasgow in 1813. Each float was fixed in a horizontal spindle to which was attached a cranked arm. A rod connected the crank to a ring which ran eccentric to the paddle shaft. The idea was simple, and sound, and although many other methods were tried, Buchanan's basic idea was used when feathering became universally adopted.

Unlike the screw the larger part of a paddle-wheel was always out of the water, so that the paddle shafts were set well above the water-line and the engine room was situated between the paddle-boxes. The engine room was one of the most fascinating features of the paddle steamer. The commencement of every voyage would be preceded

90

by a rush below decks of excited small boys, accompanied by their equally excited fathers. Often nothing but a low guard fence separated them from the engines, and here they could watch while god-like creatures controlled their mighty charges.

Telegraph bells rang, shiny brass levers were pushed and pulled, and slowly the massive cranks would begin to rise and fall. Silently at first, then rising to a rumbling, pounding crescendo. This was a Mecca of steam, a glorious place to be, awe-inspiring, wondrous, a sight and sound that has gone forever.

Chapter Ten

THE BONNY BOATS OF CLYDE

After the *Comet* — Resistance to the Railway Companies by
private owners — David McBrayne — Robert Campbell — Peter
and Alex Campbell move south — Caledonian Railway forms
Steam Packet Company — The Clyde fleets — Racing incidents —
Railway Companies merge — Services between wars.

THE story of the paddle steamer started on the River
Clyde—and throughout every phase of that story, Scotland's major river has played an important part. Here
the tiny *Comet* plied, and on the river's banks the
shipbuilding industry moved from sail to steam, turning
out the finest paddle steamers in the world. Clyde-built
steamers had the reputation of being strongly constructed,
reliable and comfortable. Scottish marine engineers were
always in advance of their contemporaries elsewhere, and
Clydesiders came to expect the best in this mode of
travel.

Once the *Comet* had overcome the initial opposition to
the steamboat, the ever-practical Scots began to realise its
advantages. Steamer services were introduced to serve
many towns, villages and hamlets that lay on the shores
and islands of the Firth of Clyde.

The river itself is navigable right into the heart of
Glasgow and during the early part of the nineteenth
century the steamer services were the easiest and quickest
way to travel to such places as Greenock, Wemyss Bay and
Ayr. Furthermore, the Glaswegians began to discover
the natural beauty of the Clyde coast and pleasure

excursions became a popular pastime. Then the railways came.

At first the steamboat owners saw this as a threat to their business, especially when lines were extended from Glasgow to the Clydebank towns. But it was soon realised that the railways could only extend so far, and there were many places that were inaccessible to them. The steamer operators adjusted their schedules so that the steamers ran in connection with the train services, thus providing a network of routes serving some of the most remote parts of Scotland.

The railway companies also saw the advantages of extending their services with onward travel by steamer, but the Government were opposed to ownership of steamers by the railway companies and several early attempts by them to set up steamboat companies were short-lived.

The Glasgow, Paisley and Greenock Railway Company were the first to try, in 1844. From 1841 the Bute Steam Packet Company had run its steamers in connection with the railway and the G.P. & G.R. took over their two ships, the *Isle of Bute* and the *Maid of Bute*. They extended the fleet with the addition of the *Pilot, Pioneer* and *Petrel,* but the competition with the private owners, coupled with their lack of experience, forced them to sell out in 1846.

Arrangements were made with several companies to provide services in connection with the railways, and this system worked quite well for a number of years. Another attempt to operate railway steamers was made in 1852 by the Railway Steam Packet Company, but they lasted for only two years and the trade reverted to the private owners once again.

It was nearly twenty years before a railway company again ventured into the steamboat business. This time success seemed assured, for the private companies had recently suffered a blow when the Greenock and Wemyss

Bay Railway Bill was passed by the House of Lords. The Wemyss Bay Steamboat Company, a subsidiary of the new railway, was formed in 1865 with four steamers. They were intended to provide a link between Wemyss Bay and Rothesay, on the Isle of Bute, but poor management and inexperience combined to bring about their downfall. The vessels were slow and in their first season failed to keep to the timetables. Efforts were made to improve the situation, but in 1869 the steamers were withdrawn and the Company wound up.

The North British Railway Company inaugurated a steamer service in 1866 running from Helensburgh, on the northern shore of the Firth, to Ardrishaig, in the Western Highlands. This is a distance of over 100 miles and two paddle steamers, the *Dandie Dinmont* and the *Meg Merrilies,* were built by A. & J. Inglis to work on the route. A financial scandal within the parent company was a major factor in the failure of the service, and in consequence the *Meg Merrilies* was sold and her sister ship restricted to sailings to Dunoon and Holy Loch. Unlike the other railway concerns, however, the North British managed to weather the storm and maintained a small fleet for several years. Their contribution to the Clyde services at the beginning were small, and it was not until the coming of the Caledonian Railway in 1888 that the position of the private companies was seriously challenged. Its arrival opened the period that has been referred to as the Golden Age of the Clyde steamers.

Before looking at the events of that period it is worth taking a closer look at some of the companies, and their ships, who had withstood the threat of the railways. David McBrayne had been a junior partner in the shipping firm of David Hutchinson and Co., and in 1877 he became the virtual controller. Two years later the firm became David McBrayne Ltd. The McBrayne fleet was graced by one of the most famous paddle steamers in Britain, the *Columba*.

She was built in 1878 when David McBrayne's monopoly of the West Highlands seaboard was challenged by the Glasgow and Inverary Steamboat Company's *Lord of the Isles*.

The *Columba* provided luxury travel designed to attract the custom of high society. She was the ship in which the 'best people' travelled on their way to their estates and shooting lodges.

Built by J. & G. Thomson of Clydebank she was 301.4ft long with a beam of 27.1ft, the largest paddle steamer to operate on the Clyde. The deck saloons extended to the full width of the hull and were lavishly furnished. A barber's shop and a post office were among the special facilities provided. In many ways she was old-fashioned in design. The curved bow and square stern belonged to a period of some ten years earlier, and her oscillating engines were of a type long since abandoned by the majority of shipbuilders. Nevertheless, she had a top speed of 19 knots, which she could achieve with complete smoothness. Her high-arched paddle-boxes, and two funnels set fore and aft, gave her a stately appearance, and possibly it was this that appealed to her high class clientele. At any rate, she held off the challenge of the *Lord of the Isles* and served her owner for 58 years.

The *Columba* ran only during the summer season and the mail service during the winter months was maintained by the *Grenadier*.

This was another vessel that had the attractive lines associated with so many of the Clyde steamers. She had a clipper bow, with the figurehead of a Grenadier under the bowsprit, two funnels and full width saloons with large observation windows. The engines were compound oscillating, the first of this type to be built.

All-day cruises in the Firth of Clyde and along the Western Coast attracted many Glaswegians anxious to get away from the smoke and grime of the city. Unfortunately these trips were often marred by the behaviour of people who spent more time at the bar than admiring the magnificent scenery. To spare passengers this embarrassment a group of business-men decided to run a 'teetotal' ship. They formed the Firth of Clyde Steam Packet Company in 1880 and ordered a 225ft long paddle steamer from the yards of D. & W. Henderson. The ship was named *Ivanhoe* and she ran daily throughout the summer season to the Isle of Arran, calling at Bute on the way.

She was a handsome, two funnelled vessel with a long promenade deck above the main and fore saloons. The engines were two cylinder diagonal oscillating, working on a single crank.

The *Ivanhoe* came to be one of the best-loved steamers on the Clyde. Not only because it was possible to take wives and children on board in safety, but also her general appearance was of a very high standard. This was due to her master and joint owner, Captain James Williamson. He kept his ship in immaculate condition, the crew wore smart, navy-style uniforms and an atmosphere of 'class' was generated.

One of the most popular of all the private steam owners on the Clyde was Captain 'Bob' Campbell. He ran a small fleet between Broomielaw and Holy Loch in the early 'eighties, but a financial set-back caused him to sell his vessels. However, he was so popular that, with the help of friends, he was able to buy the *Meg Merrilies,* the second ship of that name built for the North British Co.

With the assistance of his sons, Peter and Alex, he rebuilt his business and in 1885 purchased a new steamer, the *Waverley*. The *Madge Wildfire* followed in 1886 and for two years the Campbells enjoyed a prosperous business. But the next bid by the railways was not far off, and the Campbells were in a vulnerable position. The Caledonian Railway Company had erected a pier just across the firth from Campbell's home base at Kilmun. The Captain did not live to face the new challenge, for on April 1888, he died at his home in Glasgow after a long illness. His funeral was on a scale unprecedented on Clydeside. The coffin was taken from Glasgow to Kilmun in the *Madge Wildfire* and was carried to the graveyard at Kilmun Church by members of the crew. Notabilities from all walks of life were at the graveside to pay homage to the man who had gained a tremendous reputation for honesty, generosity and kindness.

Peter and Alex Campbell carried on the business, but they were astute businessmen and saw the futility of trying to compete with the now well-established railways. Within a few months of their father's death they had sold the *Meg Merrilies* and the *Madge Wildfire* to their new rivals. They moved south, to Bristol, taking the *Waverley* with them, and we shall pick up their story again in later chapters.

The departure of the Campbell brothers was greeted with sorrow and dismay by the Clydesiders, and it was in an atmosphere of antagonism that the Caledonian Railway Company set about inaugurating their steamer services. To begin with the Company had tried to get the co-operation of the private owners, but although a few agreed, the services that they offered were not good enough. The purchase of the two Campbell ships provided a nucleus of a railway steamer fleet, but the Clyde Steamship Owners Association petitioned Parliament against the Caledonian Railway (Steam Vessels) Bill.

They put forward some powerful arguments, the most damaging being the revelation that Caledonian had already purchased two steamers without the consent of Parliament. Faced with disaster the Company resorted to a transparent subterfuge and formed an associate company to run the steamers. Under the circumstances they had no other choice, and in May 1889, the Caledonian Steam

Packet Company was formed, with Captain James Williamson, of the *Ivanhoe,* as secretary and manager.

Williamson lost no time in applying the same high standards to his new fleet as he had done on the *Ivanhoe.* The *Meg Merrilies* and the *Madge Wildfire* were repainted and decorated in a style that became the hallmark of the Caledonian steamers. The hulls were dark blue, with a sea-green underside and a broad white band at water-level.

Two gold lines were painted just below deck level and the names at the bow and stern were also in gold lettering. The paddle-boxes were white and bore an impressive red, blue and gold crest. The saloons and sponsons were pale pink, panelled in pale blue, the deck-houses were varnished teak, and bright yellow funnels completed the very smart livery.

Appropriately, the first new steamer to be ordered by the Caledonian Co. was named *Caledonia.* She was launched by Captain Williamson's daughter at the yards of Messrs. John Reid and Co. at Port Glasgow on the 6th May, 1889. The *Caledonia* incorporated a revolutionary new engine design consisting of two cylinders placed in tandem and working on the compound system. The two pistons had a common piston-rod which worked on a single crank. Her boilers, also, were a new innovation. There were two of them, built to the Navy pattern, and they worked under a forced draught in a closed stokehold.

The new engine arrangement was the object of some criticism, but a speed of 16 knots quickly silenced the detractors. The ship did, however, suffer from the main fault of single-cylinder engines in that the fore and aft movements of the pistons created an unpleasant surging motion.

A month after the launching of the *Caledonia* a larger ship, destined to be the flagship of the fleet, left the slipway. The *Galatea* was not only larger and faster than the *Caledonia* but she had compound diagonal engines, the first to be used in a Clyde steamer. Four navy boilers supplied the steam, which necessitated two funnels set very wide apart. So advanced were these engines that their power had apparently been underestimated, with the result that the ship could not be driven at maximum speed in safety.

The opening of the Glasgow-Gourock railway had been a great success and the railways began to push their lines further along Clydebank. In 1890 they reached Ardrossan, which meant that a relatively short crossing to Arran was now possible. For this service the Caledonian Co. put out tenders for a new vessel, to be named *Duchess of Hamilton*. The contract was awarded to Denny Bros. of Dumbarton, a firm which was busily engaged in building steamers for the Thames. The *Duchess of Hamilton* did, in fact, bear a marked resemblance to the 'Belle' steamers. She was the first Clyde steamer to have a promenade deck carried forward to the bows, a style that became characteristic of subsequent Caledonian vessels.

The new service opened on 30th May, 1890, and the *Duchess of Hamilton* immediately came up against competition from the *Scotia,* owned by Captain William Buchanan. The Caledonian steamer was considerably faster than her rival, but that did not prevent some close racing which led to several incidents.

On one occasion the two ships were racing neck and neck towards the narrow entrance of Ardrossan Harbour when the *Scotia* rammed her opponent's paddle-box causing her to nearly collide with a moored barge. An incident which now seems amusing occurred when the *Duchess of Hamilton,* anxious to keep ahead of her rival, left Brodick pier while passengers were still embarking. The gangway, with some passengers still on it, was left balanced precariously on the landing stage. The luckless victims of this hasty departure were further mortified when they had to complete their journey on the *Scotia,* for which they had to pay.

Racing between the various rival steamers was commonplace on the Clyde and collisions were frequent, the entrance to Ardrossan Harbour being a particularly hazardous point. But in addition to minor bumps between racing steamers there were a number of fatal accidents. Small boats were prone to being run down or swamped, often resulting in the drowning of the occupants.

A series of accidents of this nature led to the repositioning of the bridge forward of the funnels on many of the Clyde steamers.

Safety on board was often not of a very high standard, and from time to time passengers, including children, were lost overboard.

It is remarkable that the reckless navigation during the latter part of the nineteenth century did not lead to a disaster comparable to the *Princess Alice* tragedy on the Thames. But whereas the Thames incident of 1878 put an end to irresponsible behaviour the Clyde steamers continued to battle well into the 1900's.

While the Caledonian Company was establishing itself at the major railheads, other rivalries on other parts of the river continued.

The North British Steam Packet Company, having survived their earlier set-backs, began to modernise their fleet, the Inverary Company replaced the *Lord of the Isles* by a larger ship of the same name and David McBrayne's *Columba* still ruled the Ardrishaig service. At the start of the 1889 season it was announced that the North British steamer *Jeanie Deans* had been fitted with a surface condenser, resulting in a considerable improvement in speed. In the previous season the *Jeanie Deans* had invaded the McBrayne territory by running a special excursion to Ardrishaig, and her owners had openly challenged the *Columba* to a race. The result was a

victory for the *Jeanie Deans,* which she repeated on
another occasion during the same season. Speed, however,
was not the main requirement of the Clyde steamers.
Comfort was more important, and the *Jeanie Deans* had
no covered saloons. In 1894 she was rebuilt to remedy this
deficiency, which robbed her of her one outstanding advantage. From then on she became a very ordinary vessel,
and the North British Company sold her to an Irish firm
in 1896.

She returned to the Clyde in 1898 as the *Duchess of
York,* to join a new company, the Glasgow Steamers Ltd.
In 1904 Buchanan Steamers Ltd. purchased her and
changed her name to *Isle of Cumbrae.*

Rivals to the Caledonian Railway Company were the
Glasgow and South Western Railway, but the latter relied
on private owners to provide steamers in connection with
their rail services. In 1891 they applied for, and obtained,
permission to run their own fleet. Four steamers were
purchased from Captain Alexander Williamson, and they
also acquired the *Duchess of Hamilton* and a new vessel
was ordered for 1892. This was the *Glen Sannox,* built at
the Clydebank yard of J. & G. Thomson. She was a large,
two funnelled steamer with a full length promenade deck.
Her dimensions were 260.5ft by 30.1ft, and the steel hull
was plated up to the promenade deck at the bows, a
feature which was new to Clyde steamers. The Glasgow
Company were now able to give effective opposition to
their rivals, for the new ship was larger and faster than
the *Duchess of Hamilton,* and just as comfortable.

On her trials she averaged $19\frac{1}{2}$ knots, with a maximum
of $20\frac{1}{4}$ knots, over the measured mile. The engines were
compound diagonal and were fed by one double-ended
and one Navy boiler. The *Glen Sannox* spent most of her
life on the Arran-Ardrossan run, and the train services
were improved to take full advantage of her speed. The
fastest train/steamer service was from Brodick, in the

Isle or Arran, to Glasgow, a journey of eighty minutes.

The new service brought passengers flocking back to the Glasgow and South Western. Competition with the Caledonian reached its peak in 1894, and the Marine Police Court was kept busy dealing with cases of collisions, cutting-in and other dangerous manoeuvres.

The North British Company ran the service from Craigendoran on the north bank of the river, and did not come into direct competition with the other two railway companies. Rothesay, Dunoon, Greenock and Arrochar were places mainly served by the North British steamers, with occasional excursion trips further afield.

The fleet consisted of steamers bearing the name of Sir Walter Scott's characters, *Diana Vernon, Lucy Ashton, Guy Mannering* and, in 1895, *Redgauntlet*. Built by Barclay, Curle and Company, the *Redgauntlet* was larger than any other steamer previously owned by the Company. She replaced the *Guy Mannering* on the Rothesay route and also ran excursions. It was while she was on a cruise round the Isle of Arran that the *Redgauntlet* was involved in a spectacular accident. Leaving Craigendoran on the morning of 16th August, 1899, she ran into heavy weather in the firth. The wind rose to gale force driving her close to the shore at the southern end of Arran and shortly after lunch the ship struck a submerged reef. The *Redgauntlet* was badly holed, and as the sea came pouring in she began to settle at the stern. Panic broke out among the passengers and the master, Captain McPhail, steered for the shore in order to beach his stricken vessel. He was only just in time, for as the water rose to the level of the boiler the ship went aground and an explosion was averted.

The ninety-seven passengers were rescued by local people who had come down to the beach. Fortunately the *Redgauntlet* was not a total loss, and after being refloated was repaired at a cost of £5,737. Captain McPhail was held responsible for the accident, but his prompt action in beaching the ship saved him his certificate, although the Company reduced him to the position of Mate.

At the end of the 19th century the golden age of the Clyde steamers was at its peak. The late 'nineties produced some of the finest paddle steamers ever built, and each company regularly added new steamers to their fleets. But in the early 1900's the decline started. The competition had been too fierce, too ruthless, and retrenchment was inevitable. Furthermore, the railway companies had lost favour with the public after what became known as 'the siege of Millport'.

In 1906 the Millport Town Council improved their pier facilities and raised the steamer dues to pay for them. The Caledonian and G. & S.W.R. joined forces and refused to call at Millport, which meant that the Isle of Bute was virtually cut off from the mainland. The dispute dragged on throughout the summer months and was only settled when David Lloyd-George, then President of the Board of Trade, acted as conciliator.

During the first decade of the new century the companies began to cut down the size of their fleets. Many ships were sold abroad, like the *Meg Merrilies* which went to Rio de Janeiro in 1902, and the *Galatea* who ended up at Genoa in 1906. The *Redgauntlet* went to work in the Firth of Forth in 1909, and finally to Oran in the South of France.

Against this trend Buchanan Steamers ordered a new ship in 1910. She bore the name *Eagle III*, the numeral being part of her name. By the standards of the Victorian steamers she was crudely built, with a single diagonal engine and haystack boiler, a type of installation that was long out-dated.

Nevertheless, her speed of 16½ knots was quite respectable, and her owners were well pleased with their latest purchase. Their satisfaction was short-lived, for on her first voyage the *Eagle III* developed a heavy list which lifted one paddle-wheel clear of the water. She was returned to the builders, A. & J. Inglis, who completely rebuilt the hull and the ship was relaunched in March 1911.

In the years immediately prior to the First World War there was a revival of excursion traffic. Captain John Williamson purchased a new ship in 1912 and named her *Queen Empress*. She was the last ship to go into service before the war. During the summer seasons there were regular sailings from Glasgow to the coast and something of the spirit of the golden age was recaptured. But it could not last. When war came the steamers dispersed to carry out their wartime duties in various ways. Minesweepers, troopships, boomships, some returned with honours, others did not return at all, and those that did came back to a new way of life.

In 1923 the railways merged into two major companies. The London, Midland and Scottish Railways, which included the Caledonian and G. & S.W.R., and the London North Eastern Railways, of which the North British Company became a part.

The L.M.S. expanded their fleet with turbine steamers, but in 1934 they acquired two new paddle steamers, the *Mercury (II)* and the *Caledonia (II)*. Both steamers were of an entirely new design, although the *Mercury* was built by Fairfield and the *Caledonia* by Messrs. Denny. Enclosed paddle-boxes were one of their less endearing features, elliptical funnels, one each, twin masts and cruisers sterns completed a picture which came as something of a shock to those who remembered the paddle steamers of pre-war days.

But they were efficient vessels. Powered by triple-expansion engines, which gave a maximum speed of around 17 knots, they could accommodate over 1,000 passengers and gave good service on the Greenock, Gourock and Wemyss Bay route.

Two years later the L.M.S. ordered two more paddle steamers from the Fairfield Shipbuilding and Engineering Company. They were of similar design to the *Mercury* and *Caledonia,* but had two funnels and their lines were generally more pleasing. A new innovation was storage space for motor-cars. Both ships bore the names of predecessors, *Jupiter* and *Juno*.

The L.N.E.R. perpetuated the name *Jeanie Deans* in 1931 with a Fairfield-built paddle steamer which was the largest to have operated from Craigendoran. Her predecessor had the reputation of being a 'racer', and the new ship carried on the tradition with a maximum speed of 18.5 knots. Triple-expansion engines were fitted, and two funnels, which originally were rather short causing the deck to be showered with cinders if the wind was in the wrong quarter.

The most unusual paddler to operate on the Clyde, or anywhere in Britain, was the *Talisman*. The L.N.E.R. put her into service in 1935 and she was the first direct-acting diesel-electric paddle vessel in the world.

Her four diesel engines drove D.C. generators which supplied current to a double-armature electric motor situated on the paddleshaft. Externally she resembled orthodox paddle steamers, but her outstanding feature was economy of running. 100 miles could be covered on 1.47 tons of liquid fuel, and she could run on three or even two engines.

This then, was the situation just prior to the Second World War. Gone were the days of the racers, the railway companies were working in harmony, competently and rationally, providing excellent steamer services in the best traditions of the Clyde. Perhaps some of their ships were less 'bonny' than some that the older generation remembered, but nowhere in Britain is there such a complex of islands and waterways, requiring reliable, fast and comfortable vessels to maintain communications. In this respect the paddle steamers have served the Clydesiders well, and are remembered by them with affection.

Although this chapter has been about the Clyde paddle steamers it would not be right to leave Scotland without mentioning the steamers of Loch Lomond. The history of steam navigation on the Loch goes back to 1817 when David Napier, cousin of the famous marine engineer Robert Napier, purchased the *Marion*. This tiny wooden paddler sailed from Glasgow to Loch Lomond via the Leven. She was a mere 60ft in length with a beam of 13ft, and was powered by a 20 h.p. side-lever engine. The *Marion* operated for eight years without opposition, but Napier's success had not gone unnoticed. In 1825 the Loch Lomond Steamboat Company was formed with a view of capturing some of the trade. With their new steamer, *The Lady of the Lake,* they attacked Napier's trade with a vengeance, cutting fares so much that before long they were in financial difficulties. After 1828 Napier was again on his own, and in 1832 he replaced the *Marion* with the *Euphrosyne.*

Happily the next move was one of amalgamation rather than opposition. The New Loch Lomond Steamboat Company was formed in 1845 with David Napier as a partner, and this Company regularly added new steamers, and replaced the old ones, until 1888 when they were taken over by North British Company. A further eight years passed before the next change, which came when the North British interests were transferred to the Dumbarton and Balloch Joint Line Committee. At that time there were four steamers on the Loch, the *Prince of Wales, Prince Consort, The Queen* and the *Empress,* and in 1898 the new owners enlarged the fleet with the addition of two new steamers, the *Prince George* and the *Princess May.* They were sister-ships, built to the same dimensions as *The Queen* and *Empress,* and were fitted with similar engines, the rather out-dated non-compound diagonal twin-cylinder type. In 1914 two more sister-ships arrived at the Loch, but they were not new, and had journeyed far. The *Princess Patricia* and *Queen Mary* had been built for the short-lived London County Council project in 1905, and were originally named *Shakespeare* and *Earl Godwin*.

The *Queen Mary* was badly damaged by fire shortly after her arrival and spent several years languishing in her berth at Balloch until she was broken up in 1928.

The 1923 grouping of the major railway companies brought another change of ownership, although it was ten years before the steamers were transferred to the control of Group 4 Committee of the L.M.S. and L.N.E.R. Between the wars the services were maintained principally by four steamers, but after the Second War a new steamer was ordered. The *Maid of the Loch* was launched in 1953, and was the last paddle steamer to be built in Britain. She is still in service, and it is quite possible that before long she will be the only paddle steamer sailing in British waters. It is fitting, therefore, that her story be more fully told in the final chapter of this book.

Chapter Eleven

PADDLE STEAMERS OF THE
NORTH-WEST COAST

Mersey to North Wales services — Loss of the *Rothsay Castle* — Liverpool and North Wales Steamship Company — *La Marguerite* on the North Wales service — Mersey Ferries—collisions — Isle of Man Steam Packet Company — Lancashire coastal paddle steamers.

NORTH WALES, the Isle of Man and Merseyside have been well-served by paddle steamers, and regular services in that area began in the first quarter of the nineteenth century.

The Mersey to North Wales service commenced in 1821 when a small paddler, the *Cambria,* sailed from Liverpool to Bagilt on the 4th June. The following year the first steamer crossing from Liverpool to the Menai Straits was made by the *Albion.* The St. George Steam Packet Company, whose main interests were the mail services to Ireland, Scotland and the Isle of Man, put a vessel, the *Prince Llewelyn,* on the North Wales service, and she was later joined by the *St. David.* Both vessels had previously operated on the Isle of Man route, and the *Prince Llewelyn* in particular was not noted for its excellent passenger facilities. The two steamers sailed regularly from St. Georges Dock to Beaumaris and Bangor, the voyage taking six hours.

In 1843 the City of Dublin Steam Packet Company took over the North Wales service from the St. George Co. and in 1880 the service changed hands again to become the Liverpool, Llandudno and Welsh Coast

Steamship Company. By now the quality of passenger facilities had begun to improve, as one would expect with successive take-overs. The pattern in the North-West was very much the same as in other parts of the country. Small companies merged together, or were taken over by larger companies until in each area only a few companies emerged, with names that were, and in some cases still are, famous in British maritime history. There were, however, many 'one-man, one-ship' concerns which tried to compete with the large companies. Often these ships were bought when they were almost due for the breakers yards. They were patched up and put into service with the object of making a quick profit. One such vessel was the *Rothsay Castle,* whose tragic loss was a direct result of financial greed, bad seamanship and gross stupidity.

The *Rothsay Castle* ran on the Liverpool-Menai Straits service in the same period as the *Prince Llewelyn* and the *Albion.* She was a tiny vessel with engines of a mere 34 n.h.p. and had been built on the Clyde in 1816. After several years' service in that area she was purchased by a Mr. Watson of Liverpool. Apart from the fact that she was almost worn out, the vessel had been built for navigation in the sheltered waters of the Clyde and was quite unsuited for the heavy weather which is often encountered in the Irish Sea.

On August 17th, 1831, the *Rothsay Castle* was scheduled to sail from Liverpool at 10 a.m. for Beaumaris. Between 130 and 150 passengers were on board and the start was delayed for nearly an hour while a coach was loaded on board. As soon as the ship was clear of the mouth of the Mersey she was in trouble. A fresh wind whipped up the sea and the tiny engines struggled to make headway. By lunch time the passengers, many of whom were violently seasick, were becoming alarmed and several people approached the Captain asking him to turn back. Their requests were rejected with scornful arrogance, and it was quite obvious that the man was drunk.

As the vessel rolled and pitched in the heavy seas, water began to force its way through the paddleshaft bearings. The engine room was soon awash, and there was a danger that the boiler fires would be extinguished. Little Ormes Head was reached just after eight o'clock in the evening, and the four miles to Great Ormes Head took two hours. In eleven hours only thirty six miles had been covered. The water was now flooding the cabins, and the passengers were taking turns at the pumps in a desperate effort to keep the engineroom clear. But although the boiler fires were still burning the coal had been rendered useless. Steam pressure fell and the ship made less headway than before.

The first sight of land came just before midnight. It was Puffin Island, at the entrance to the Menai Straits, but before the ship could reach safety she touched bottom and within seconds was completely aground.

At the mercy of the pounding waves she rapidly filled with water, and still the Captain maintained that there was no danger. He made no attempt to call for assistance and in fact, was unable to do so, for the ship had no signalling apparatus of any kind.

The *Rothsay Castle* now began to break up. The tall funnel crashed to the deck taking the mainmast with it, and from that time on the captain and his mate were not seen again. The passengers took to the sea, using whatever wreckage they could find to cling to. Some tried to swim to Puffin Island, but when the Beaumaris lifeboat put out in the early hours of the morning only 23 survivors were found.

Like the *Princess Alice* disaster 47 years later, the tragedy led to a tightening up of the rules and regulations that governed the building and maintenance of paddle steamers, and a lighthouse was built at Penmon.

The major company to emerge on the Liverpool-North

Wales excursion trade was the Liverpool and North Wales Steamship Company Ltd. Its ancestral line is complicated, evolving as it did, from a number of mergers and take-overs. It was formed in 1891 to acquire the interests of the New North Wales Steamship Company, which was part of the Fairfield Shipbuilding and Engineering Company organisation. The N.N.W.S. Co. had already absorbed the Liverpool, Llandudno and Welsh Coast Steamboat Company, which in turn had taken over the North Wales service of the City of Dublin Steam Packet Company. The name Fairfield appears often in the story of the paddle steamer. As one of Britain's major shipbuilding concerns many paddle steamers left their yards on the Clyde, and it is not surprising that a steamship company should be one of their many ventures. The Steamship Company started business in 1890 with two ships, the *Paris* and the *St. Tudno*. The *Paris* had already been in service for 15 years on the cross-channel route between Newhaven and Dieppe. She was a good sea boat, 220ft in length and 25.2ft in beam, with a set of compound oscillating engines.

Even so, her 13 knots was too slow for the cross-Channel service and when she was sold back to her builders, she was reconditioned and re-boilered.

The *St. Tudno* had been built in 1889 as the *Cobra*. She was owned by Messrs. G. and J. Burns who ran the ship between the Clyde and Belfast for one season. 264.8ft in length, 33.1ft in beam, she had a gross tonnage of 1,146. The engines were compound diagonal, giving an i.h.p. of 4,500.

The two ships offered a very comprehensive service. The *St. Tudno* sailing each day, except Sundays, at 10.30 a.m., for Llandudno, Beaumaris and Garth Ferry, and returning the same day to arrive back at 6.45 p.m. The *Paris* sailed on Fridays and Saturdays at 1.00 p.m. returning at 10.45 p.m. The merging of the Liverpool, Llandudno and Welsh Coast Steamboat Company added two ships to the fleet. The *Prince Arthur* and the *Bonnie Princess*. The *St. Tudno* was sold to the Hamburg-Amerika Company and reverted to her original name of *Cobra*.

A year later the *Paris* was sold to a German firm and renamed *Flamingo*.

A new ship had already been ordered by the N.N.W.S. Co. and when she was delivered to her new owners she bore the name of *St. Tudno II*. She was built, of course, by Fairfield and was at that time the largest and fastest steamer on the North Wales service. Her length was 265.4ft and the breadth 32.6ft. She carried 1,061 passengers and amenities included three decks, a ladies cabin, smoking room, first and second class saloons and a dining room where the catering was of a high standard. Her maximum speed of 20.4 knots was derived from diagonal compound, direct-acting engines of 5,000 i.h.p. driving a single paddleshaft.

Five years later she was joined by the *St. Elvis*. Rather smaller than the *St. Tudno* she tended to be overshadowed by her big sister, but served her owners for 35 years, except for the war years when she took up minesweeping duties.

Another small, but long-lived steamer was the *Snowdon II*. She joined the L. & N.W.S. Co. when the Snowdon Passenger Steamship Company was taken over. Launched in 1892, she too served as a minesweeper, and survived until 1931.

We now pick up the story of the famous paddle steamer *La Marguerite* once more. As previously mentioned in Chapter Five she was built by Fairfields for Palace Steamers Ltd., in 1893, and was operated by the Victoria Steamboat Association. Fairfields had an interest in both of these companies and were, in fact, virtual owners of the *La Marguerite*. Despite her great popularity, she was not a financial success, and in 1905 Fairfields transferred her to the L. & N.W.S. Co. She was a useful acquisition, her strength and size being ideal for the North Wales service. For many years she ran from Liverpool to Llandudno, Beaumaris, Bangor and Menai Bridge. During the First World War she was used as a troopship, sailing between Southampton and the French coast.

In 1919 she returned to the North West coast and went on charter to the Isle of Man Steam Packet Company, but in 1920 she was back on the North Wales service. Unfortunately the war years had left their mark, and a number of breakdowns occurred. On one occasion a rudder chain broke and the ship had to be manoeuvred by her paddles. Trouble with the paddle-wheels also occurred frequently. And so, in 1925, it was decided that she would be withdrawn at the end of the season. Her last voyage in the service of the L. & N.W.S. Co. took place on September 28th, 1925. At each port of call she was given a tumultuous welcome. Crowds thronged the piers, bands played and rockets were fired. On October 22nd she left the Mersey for the last time, bound for the breakers yards of Messrs. Ward at Briton Ferry.

Her ship's bell was presented to the City of London Rifles, who were the first troops carried by her during the war.

It now forms part of a War Memorial to the regiment in St. Sepulchre's Church, Holborn, and is rung every September at the annual re-union of the survivors.

It is inevitable that such an illustrious vessel should collect a number of stories and legends during her lifetime. Once, when she was operating on the London to France service, she was rumoured to have been sunk, with a heavy loss of life. This story arose from an overheard remark by the Harbour Master who reported that '*La Marguerite* had gone down', meaning that she had gone down the river. Her size led to some amusing stories, such as the case of the American passenger who thought that

8   113

he was on the White Star liner *Baltic*. It was only when he asked a steward to show him to his cabin that he discovered his mistake.

The *La Marguerite* was the largest paddle steamer owned by the L. & N.W.S. Co.

Three years after she joined the fleet the company was encountering strong competition from the Mersey Trading Company, and to combat this they bought the *Southampton*. She had been used for short runs on the South Coast and carried 272 passengers. When she joined the North Wales service she was renamed *St. Elien*. 150.1ft in length with compound diagonal engines of 84 n.h.p. she was a light craft, but nevertheless gave good service until she was withdrawn in 1915.

The last paddler to go into service with the L. & N.W.S. Co., was the *St. Trillo*. Built in 1876 as the *Carisbrooke*, for the Isle of Wight service, she continued under that name with the Colwyn Bay and Liverpool Steamship Company, then joined the Mersey Trading Company who re-named her *Rhos Trevor*. In 1909 the L. & N.W.S. Co. put her on the North Wales service alongside the *St. Elien*. After serving as a minesweeper during the war she returned to North Wales in 1919, where she remained until she was sold to a Spanish owner who re-named her *San Telmo*.

A few months before her departure for Spain the *St. Trillo* was involved in an incident when she struck a rock while returning from a trip to Caernarvon. Most of the passengers were taken off by motor boats, and when the tide lifted her clear she proceeded to Port Dinorwic with some passengers still on board.

The Liverpool and North Wales Steamship Company started to introduce steam turbine engines into their fleet just before the First World War, and several of them carried the names of the old paddle steamers, but they have no place in this book, and at this point we turn to the area which is at the centre of all the North West coast services. The Mersey.

A glance at the map shows that the Mersey is very different in character to both the Thames and the Clyde. At its mouth, where stands Liverpool and Birkenhead, it is barely ¾ mile wide, but further up river it widens to about three miles, before narrowing again between Widnes and Runcorn.

The river is fast flowing and at times becomes very turbulent. To cross this stretch of water requires powerful, rugged craft, and the Mersey ferry steamers were just that, with no pretentions to grace or beauty.

On Merseyside all roads lead to Liverpool, and ferry services to the city ran from eleven points on the south bank. The oldest of these, the Woodside Ferry, was instituted under a Royal Charter granted by Edward III in 1332. The early history of steamboats on these ferries is somewhat confused, as many of them were run by private individuals and it was not until the local Corporations of Wallasey and Birkenhead took over that accurate records were kept. The first paddle steamer to operate on the Mersey was not a ferry but a packet. In 1815 Lieutenant Colin Watson brought the *Elizabeth* from the Clyde, where she had been built in 1812, to ply between Runcorn and Liverpool. Apart from being the first steamer on the Mersey she was the first to make the journey from the Clyde, and was also the second practical steamboat in Europe, the first being the *Comet*.

Like her famous predecessor she was not an instant success and ran for only one year, between 1815 and 1816. The *Elizabeth* was built by John Ward of Glasgow and had an 8 h.p. engine designed by John Thomson. She was a wooden paddler, 57ft long by 12ft beam.

After 1816 a few privately owned paddle steamers ran from Runcorn, including the *Duke of Wellington,* the first Mersey-built steamer which was constructed at

Runcorn by Walter Wright. About 1824 the Runcorn
Steam Packet Company was formed, and operated six
paddle steamers over a number of years. The packet
service lapsed after the arrival of the railway.

The first steam ferry was introduced in 1816. This was
the *Princess Charlotte* which ran from Eastham to Liverpool. In 1817 a rather odd-looking craft, the *Etna,* operated between Princes Pier, Liverpool and Tranmere. The
Etna had two hulls, decked over, with a single paddle-
wheel between. She was designed by George La French,
a Danish hotelier in Birkenhead.

The Woodside Ferry began to use paddle steamers in
1822 with the *Royal Mail,* and in the same year the
Seacombe went into service on the Seacombe Ferry. Two
iron-built vessels, the *Invincible* and the *Tiger,* were
employed at Seacombe, between 1825 and 1845, in
addition to six wooden paddlers. When New Brighton was
developed as a pleasure resort around 1830 a summer
service to Liverpool was maintained by the *Fairy* and the
Queen of Beauty.

Apart from the Wallasey and Birkenhead ferries a
number of others came into being during the 19th century.
These included the Rock Ferry, New Ferry, Monks
Ferry and the Eastham Ferry. Eastham was developed in
much the same way as New Brighton, and the developers,
Eastham Ferry Pleasure Gardens and Hotel Company,
operated a fleet of nine steamers. Their first vessel, the
Onyx, was bought in 1897 from Great Eastern Railways,
who had operated her under the name of *Norfolk* on the
Harwich-Felixstowe-Ipswich summer excursion service.

She was later joined by the *Ruby, Sapphire* and *Pearl,*
three very functional vessels with similar bow and stern
and perpendicular funnel, which gave them a 'paper-
boat-like' appearance.

With so many ships criss-crossing the river, often in the
path of sea-going vessels moving in and out of port, it is

not surprising that there were a number of collisions.

The most serious accident that ever occurred on the Mersey involved the *Gem,* owned by the Wallasey Local Government Board. On November 26th, 1898, she was crossing from Seacombe in dense fog at about 9.30 a.m. There was a strong flood tide running which carried the *Gem* off her course and across the bows of the sailing vessel *Bowfell,* which was anchored in mid-river. The ferry struck the bowsprit of the *Bowfell* which knocked over the funnel. The *Gem* was not seriously damaged, but the suddenness of the incident created a panic among the passengers and many were pushed overboard. Fifteen lives were lost, and at the subsequent inquiry blame was attached to the Wallasey Board for not giving their captains discretionary powers to stop running in dangerous conditions.

The early ferry steamers had little in the way of protection for passengers, probably because the journey was so short that it was not thought to be worthwhile. In 1853 however, the *Woodside* was introduced which had what was described as a 'glass saloon'. The *Woodside* was also involved in a collision in 1857, when she struck the anchor of the *Fairy* and began to fill rapidly. Passengers were transferred to the *Tiger* and the *Woodside* managed to reach Princes Basin, where she sank. A deck saloon was also a feature of the *Chester* of 1863. This vessel had an extreme length for a ferry boat, 150ft, the amount of traffic using the ferry piers making it difficult to berth a ship of any greater length.

In the 1890's both the Wallasey and Birkenhead ferries began to use twin-screw vessels, although the Birkenhead Corporation reverted to a paddler in 1894 with the *Birkenhead III.* The Wallasey Corporation acquired two steel paddle steamers in 1896, the *John Herron* and the *Pansy,* and these were the last of that type.

About forty miles off the Lancashire coast lies the Isle

of Man. This distance, combined with the notorious weather conditions that are sometimes encountered in the Irish Sea, necessitated the use of large vessels, and some of the largest and most handsome paddle steamers seen in the North West were used by the Isle of Man Steam Packet Company.

The first steam vessel to visit the island was the Runcorn packet, *Elizabeth*. Until 1829 services to the island were poor, and in that year the Manxmen decided to form their own company. The company is still in existence, and during its history has avoided mergers, take-overs and other complications. By doing so it must be unique among shipping companies in the United Kingdom. The Company's pioneer steamer was the *Mona's Isle,* built on the Clyde in 1830. She was constructed of wood and had a two cylinder side-lever engine designed by Robert Napier. Her clipper bow and long bowsprit, tall masts and slender funnel made her a handsome vessel, and the Company were well pleased with their purchase.

The crossing to Liverpool took eight hours, and as soon as the service was inaugurated strong competition was offered by the St. George Company. They matched their *Sophia Jane* against *Mona's Isle* on her maiden voyage and won a narrow victory. This was the only time that a St. George Company vessel managed to beat the Isle of Man vessel, and in 1831 they gave up the struggle, the *Sophia Jane* moving on to greater glory (see Chapter Four).

For the winter season the Company purchased a smaller and slightly faster vessel than the *Mona's Isle.* Built by the same contractors, John Ward & Co., and fitted with a Napier side-lever engine, the *Mona* went into service in 1832. The *Queen of the Isle* followed in 1834, and with these vessels operating an exclusive service the prosperity of the Company seemed assured. In 1835, however, an internal upset among the directors resulted in a breakaway company being formed which threatened the first opposition since the St. George Company had retired from the field.

A number of ex-directors of the Isle of Man Company, and a few sympathetic shareholders, founded the Isle of Man and Liverpool Shipping Company. They ordered a new ship, the *Monarch,* and chartered the *Clyde* to inaugurate their service. Feelings ran high between the two companies, but with only one ship the concern could not hope to survive and it collapsed in 1837.

In 1842 the last wooden paddler was built, and is worthy of mention as it was the only vessel to be constructed for the Company on the island. Named *King Orry* she had Napier side-lever engines of 180 n.h.p. and performed the Liverpool to Douglas crossing in seven hours.

The first iron paddler, the *Ben-My-Chree,* was built by Robert Napier in 1845, and was fitted with the engines from the *Queen of the Isle.*

During the next twenty years several ships joined the fleet, some of them replacements for the earlier steamers. One of particlar interest was the *Mona's Isle II.*

She was the first of the Company's vessels to be fitted with oscillating engines. The remarkable thing about this steamer was that after 23 years' service she was reconstructed as a twin-screw vessel. Her name was changed to *Ellan Vannin* and she served for a further 26 years before being lost in a storm with her entire crew.

Mona's Isle III was also an unusual vessel, but for a very different reason. When she was delivered to the Company in 1882 she was the biggest ship that they had ever owned. 1,500 tons gross, 330ft in length with a beam of 38.1ft., she was the Company's first steel ship and their first with compound oscillating engines. The details of these engines make interesting reading, for they were of staggering proportions. The high pressure cylinder was

65 inches in diameter, and the low pressure cylinder 112 inches. The stroke was 90 inches. Quite apart from the tremendous feat of engineering that this represented, it should be remembered that these were oscillating cylinders, and the sight of those massive units swinging on their trunnions must have been most impressive.

Such was the size of the pistons that it was necessary to have two piston rods to each piston, and these were 10 inches diameter. Steam was supplied to the H.P. cylinder at 90lb per square inch. *Mona's Isle III* plied on the Liverpool-Douglas service for thirty-three years, until the Admiralty purchased her in 1915 for net-laying duties. After the war she was broken up at Morecambe by T. W. Ward Limited.

After the introduction of *Mona's Isle III,* until the end of the century, the Isle of Man fleet was complemented by the addition of some of the finest paddle steamers on the North West coast, or indeed anywhere. In 1835, *Mona's Queen II* arrived as a consort to *Mona's Isle III.* Only slightly smaller than her sister she too had compound oscillating engines, but with four cylinders instead of two. The cylinders worked in pairs on two cranks, the H.P. cylinders being horizontal and the L.P.'s vertical. The i.h.p. was 5,000.

Competition was again encountered in 1887, this time of a much more serious nature than that offered by the ill-fated Isle of Man and Liverpool Shipping Company.

As we have seen earlier in this chapter the Fairfield Shipbuilding and Engineering Company made a practice of sponsoring shipping companies, using vessels of their own manufacture. This time it was the Isle of Man, Liverpool and Manchester Steamship Company, who entered the field with two Fairfield-built steamers, the *Queen Victoria* and the *Prince of Wales.* The two ships were of identical dimensions 330.5ft in length by 39.1ft beam and had compound diagonal engines of 6,500 i.h.p.

There were two cylinders each 112 inches in diameter, but not oscillating as in the *Mona's Isle III*. The *Prince of Wales* was reported as having covered the seventy miles from Rock Light to Douglas in two hours, 59 minutes, an average speed of 23½ knots. During the season of 1887 a price-cutting war raged between the two companies, but in the end common-sense prevailed and the new concern sold its fleet to their rivals.

The Company's ships reached the peak of design in 1897 with their last, and largest, paddle steamer.

Empress Queen, 360ft in length, with a gross tonnage of 2,000, was built by Fairfields and was fitted with compound diagonal engines producing 10,000 i.h.p. (1,290 n.h.p.). These engines had three cylinders, one H.P. and two L.P., each having a stroke of 7ft, and driving onto three cranks. This tremendous power gave the ship a top speed of 21½ knots. The *Empress Queen* served as a troopship during the First World War, but in 1919 she was lost when she stranded on the Isle of Wight in thick fog.

At the turn of the century the Company modified its policy of having ships built to their own specification. Their first screw steamer was acquired from the London and South West Railway Company, and in 1903 their last paddler, *Mona III,* formerly the *Calais-Douvre II,* was purchased from Liverpool and Douglas Steamers Ltd. She had originally been employed by the London, Chatham and Dover Railway Company on their cross-Channel service, and only stayed with the Isle of Man Company until 1909, when she was broken up at Briton Ferry.

It would be unpardonable to end this chapter without some reference to the paddle steamers which plied along the Lancashire coast from Morecambe, Southport and Blackpool. Regular services did not commence until the latter part of the nineteenth century, although in the

121

Morecambe area the *Helvellyn,* owned by the Furness Railway Company, commenced operations in 1842. The *Morecambe Queen* appeared in 1853, followed by the *Queen of the Bay* in 1867. The Morecambe Steamboat Company Ltd., had a small, flush-decked paddle steamer, the *Roses,* and the *Express,* a steel paddler of 426 gross tons.

Several companies operated from Blackpool, the principal concern being the Blackpool Passenger Steamboat Company Ltd. Their first vessel was the *Bickerstaffe,* of 1879, and their second, the *Queen of the North,* had an unusual engine design, there being four cylinders, two fixed and two oscillating.

Southport appears to have had only one steamship company, which traded under the curious name of Southport Steam Packet and Floating Bath Company. They owned two vessels, the *Wasp,* built in 1858, and the *Pioneer* of unknown origin.

Chapter Twelve

WEST COUNTRY PADDLE STEAMERS

Bristol Channel — The arrival of P & A Campbell — The
Campbell fleet — South Devon steamers—the Campbell
monopoly — River Dart steamers.

THE principal steamer services in the West Country
operated in the Bristol Channel and River Avon, and on
the South Devon and Cornish coasts, including the rivers
Tamar and Dart.

In the Bristol Channel the now familiar pattern was
repeated; keen competition between small concerns in the
early days, followed by the emergence of a giant with a
virtual monopoly. In this case the giant was one of the
biggest names in British coastal waters, P & A Campbell.

The name of Campbell was already well known on the
Clyde in 1888, but competition on Scotland's river was
fierce, and with the coming of the railways threatened to
become even more so. In the previous year a Bristol
syndicate had chartered Robert and Alexander Campbell's paddle steamer, the *Waverley,* and after the death
of Robert Campbell his two sons, Peter and Alec,
recognised that the Bristol Channel trade was ripe for
development.

They sold two of their vessels, the *Meg Merrilies* and
Madge Wildfire, to the Caledonian Railway Company,
and, taking the *Waverley* with them, moved south to
Bristol.

Before following the fortunes of the Campbells it is worth looking back to the beginnings of steamer navigation in the West. The first steamer recorded at Bristol was the *Charlotte,* owned by a Mr. Theodore Lawrence. In June 1813, the *Charlotte* commenced to ply from Bristol to Bath, and was joined in 1815 by the *Hope.* There then followed a succession of one-ship concerns, some operating from the North Devon coast and others from the Welsh ports such as Cardiff, Barry and Swansea.

One of the first fleets of any size was that founded by James W. Pockett, a Swansea shipbroker who was the agent for two paddle steamers, the *Lord Beresford* and the *Prince of Wales.* In 1856 Pockett bought the *Lord Beresford,* and acquired the *Prince of Wales* the following year.

The two ships plied between Swansea and Bristol, and in 1858 the fleet was enlarged by the purchase of the *Henry Southam,* which ran from Swansea to London.

Before his death, in 1880, James Pockett bought two more ships, the *Ruby* and the *Velindra,* and after his death the *Velindra* was sold to Captain William Pockett who founded the Bristol Channel Steam Packet Company Ltd. In 1890 Captain Pockett died, and the business was taken over by two Bristol businessmen, who renamed it Pockett's Bristol Channel Steam Packet Company.

The *Velindra* did well at first, but later met competition from other vessels which had superior passenger facilities. To meet this the Company purchased the *Brighton* in 1894, and, just prior to the first war, she was joined by the ex-G.S.N. steamer *Mavis.* After the war the Company had no paddle steamers left and they concentrated on cargo carrying with screw vessels.

Before the Campbells set up their office in Bristol there appeared in the port a paddle steamer which attracted a great deal of attention. It had been announced in the press that a new vessel, luxuriously appointed and with many new passenger facilities, would commence excursion trips

from Bristol to Ilfracombe on May 22nd, 1886. 10,000
people are said to have gathered on the quayside at the
old Drawbridge to see this wonderful new ship, the
Bonnie Doon.

In fact she was not all that new, and in some ways far
from wonderful. She had been built in 1876 on the Clyde,
where she ran for five years between Glasgow and Ayr.
During this time she earned a reputation for mechanical
breakdowns, which led to the unhappy nickname of
'Bonnie Breakdoon'. The Liverpool, Llandudno and Welsh
Coast Steamboat Company had her for a year, and then
she returned to the Clyde in the service of the Wemyss
Bay Steamboat Company.

Nevertheless, the Bristolians were pleased to see her.
Prior to her arrival steamboat excursions had been run
by various craft, including paddle tugs and cattle-boats,
and the arrival of a saloon steamer promised an end to
uncomfortable travel. The Bristol Steam Yachting and
Excursion Company operated the *Bonnie Doon* on charter
from her Scottish owners. The driving force behind the
Company was a Miss Kate Hedges, licensee of a public
house called the General Draper, and she made herself
responsible for all catering on board.

The *Bonnie Doon* was a great success in the new
venture, which led to her purchase by four Bristol businessmen. At that time she was the biggest paddle steamer
to have operated in those waters, 218ft in length with a
20ft beam, and was driven by a 96 n.h.p. single cylinder
diagonal engine. She had an open foredeck and a very
smart, red plush upholstered saloon situated aft. In 1890
she was transferred to Messrs. Edwards, Robertson and
Co., and in 1899 became part of the P & A Campbell fleet.

Campbells ran her for fourteen years, including service
on the South Coast, where we shall meet her again in a
later chapter.

The arrival of the Campbells in the Bristol area, while

causing some concern among local shipowners, must have been greeted with enthusiasm by the majority of Bristolians. Alexander Campbell had visited the area the year before as master of the *Waverley,* and both he and his ship had proved to be very popular. The *Waverley* was a handsome vessel, with a deck saloon aft (in 1889 a foredeck saloon was added) and a single funnel and mast. Her engines were single cylinder diagonal giving a nominal horsepower of 99. In her first season at Bristol she ran in direct competition with the *Bonnie Doon,* and was the faster of the two. Her success encouraged the Campbells to buy larger and better ships, but the *Waverley* served the Company until the First World War when she operated for a while on the Cardiff-Weston ferry. In 1917 she was called up for minesweeping duties, which she carried out in the Bristol Channel under the name of H.M.S. *Way.* After the war she was demobilised but was in such poor condition that she was scrapped in 1920.

So popular was the *Waverley* that at the end of her 1889 season Captain Campbell was presented with a silver salver, the result of a collection held on board by season ticket-holders. This show of appreciation led the Campbells to order a new ship, the first to be designed for the Bristol Channel. Her name was the *Ravenswood,* and the order was placed with the builders of the *Waverley,* Messrs. Hutson and Corbett. It is interesting to note that the name was taken from the works of Sir Walter Scott, as were the *Meg Merrilies, Madge Wildfire* and *Waverley.* *Ravenswood* was originally fitted with a single diagonal engine fed by two haystack boilers. She had two saloons, one fore and one aft, and the bridge was placed abaft the two funnels. In 1909 she was refitted with compound diagonal engines and a single boiler, which dispensed for the need for two funnels.

The Campbells placed the ship on the Bristol-

Ilfracombe run, an important service which was always reserved for the Company's best ships.

As larger vessels came along she was employed on shorter routes and operated on general excursions from Bristol and the South Wales ports. As H.M.S. *Ravenswood* she carried out minesweeping duties between 1915 and 1919, and between the wars served for a time on the South Coast. In 1941 she was back in Admiralty Grey, once more as a minesweeper, until 1945 when she was re-sold to P & A Campbell. After an extensive refit she returned to her pre-war duties, but in 1955 it was found that major hull repairs were required and she was broken up at Newport at the end of that year.

By 1893 the competition in the Bristol Channel had settled down between two companies, P & A Campbell and the Cardiff-based firm of Edwards, Robertson and Co. So intense was the struggle that in June of that year the *Ravenswood* collided with the Cardiff company's *Lorna Doone* as they raced to be first at Weston pier.

Campbells next step in the fight for supremacy was to order three new ships, the *Westward Ho!*, *Cambria* and *Britannia*.

The *Westward Ho!* was delivered from the yards of S. McKnight and Co. in 1894, and was placed under the command of Captain Alexander Campbell. On her trials she had recorded 18 knots, and when she went into service she was advertised as 'the largest, fastest ship in the Bristol Channel'. She was 225ft long, 26ft in beam and had 277 n.h.p. compound diagonal engines. Her top deck was carried forward to the bows, the first Campbell ship to be so designed. *Westward Ho!* spent most of her time in the Bristol Channel, but in common with several others of the Campbell fleet she did her stint on the South Coast. Her service in both wars mainly involved minesweeping, but in 1940 she took part in the Dunkirk evacuation when she rescued 1,686 British troops. Like so many others of her kind the strenuous activities of war service took their toll and in 1946 she was broken up at Newport.

The *Cambria* was a near sister ship to the *Westward Ho!* but with more powerful engines producing 304 n.h.p.

In the early 1900's she was claimed to be one of the fastest ships in the world, with a top speed of over 20 knots. Her career was much the same as that of the *Westward Ho!* except that she did not go to Dunkirk, and she suffered the same end in 1946.

'Queen of the Bristol Channel' was only one of the superlative descriptions of the *Britannia*. 'Greyhound of the Severn Seas' and 'Flagship of the Spotless Fleet' were two others. Similar in dimensions and speed to the *Westward Ho!* and *Cambria* she became the most popular of all the Campbell paddle steamers. Extensive refits were carried out from time to time, the last, in 1948, resulting in the fitting of a double-ended Scotch boiler, which gave her two funnels. After service in both wars she fared better than her sisters, continuing to operate until 1956.

The strengthening of the Campbell fleet had the desired effect, and shortly after the delivery of the *Britannia,* Edwards, Robertson and Co. sold out to a Mr. John Gunn.

The company had operated from Cardiff since 1883, starting with a small paddle steamer, the *Lady Margaret.* Their last vessel was the *Lady Margaret III* and she was intended to compete with the *Westward Ho!* In 1899 John Gunn sold the two remaining steamers, *Bonnie Doon* and *Scotia,* to P & A Campbell, the *Lorna Doone* having been sold to the Southampton, Isle of Wight and South of England Royal Mail Steam Packet Company earlier that year. With their main competitors out of the way P & A Campbell were able to savour the spoils of victory for a few years. But in 1905 a new challenge had to be met. The Barry Railway Company put a two-funnelled steamer, the *Devonia,* on the Bristol Channel excursion service with the avowed intention of breaking the Campbell's monopoly. The *Devonia* was a first class vessel, with a speed of 20½ knots obtained from twin cylinder diagonal engines. She raced against the *Cambria* on several occasions, but this time the battle was resolved not on the water but in the Courts.

P & A Campbell took action against the Barry Railway Company to restrain them from operating in certain areas of the Bristol Channel. After numerous adjournments the issue was finally settled in 1907, with Campbell winning the day. The *Devonia* and two other vessels were sold to the Bristol Channel Passenger Boats Ltd., which in 1911 was absorbed by P & A Campbell. The *Devonia* also served in both wars, and was at Dunkirk where she was beached and abandoned. Rumour has it that the Germans salvaged her, and that she is still in use somewhere in East Germany, but this story has never been substantiated.

One of the vessels acquired by P & A Campbell from the Bristol Channel Passenger Steamboat Company was the *Barry*. The well-known shipbuilding firm of John Brown built her for the Barry Railway Co. who used her on a three-point route between Barry, Minehead and Weston. For 34 years the *Barry* had an adventurous career, serving in many places under several different names.

Between 1914 and 1915 she was a transport ship for German prisoners of war. She then acted as a supply ship at Gallipoli, and was the last ship to leave Suvla Bay after the evacuation. Towards the end of 1917 she was renamed H.M.S. *Barryfield*. Campbells took her back after the war and until 1926 she ran under her original name. Then the Company decided to revive the name of their first ship, and the *Barry* became the *Waverley II*. The Bristol Channel and South Coast were both served by the *Waverley II* between the wars, but in 1939 she

9

underwent another change of name, this time to H.M.S. *Snaefell*. Two years later, on 5th July, 1941, she was bombed and sunk while minesweeping off the North East Coast.

The last two paddle steamers built for Campbells before the First World War were the *Glen Avon,* 1912, and the *Glen Usk,* 1914. They were twins, built at the Ailsa Company's yards at Troon, and were built to a pattern that became a standard during the 20's and 30's.

The accent was on comfort rather than speed, with spacious below-deck accommodation. The names are interesting. The Campbells had obviously not forgotten their Scottish ancestry by using the name 'Glen', even though it applied to an English and Welsh valley.

Both of the 'Glens' served in two World Wars, *Glen Avon* being lost in a gale in 1944 and *Glen Usk* surviving until 1963 when she was broken up at Passage West. In 1959 the *Glen Usk* went aground in the Avon with some 600 passengers on board and the tide falling fast. For some time there was a danger that the ship would topple over and the passengers were taken off. Fortunately she remained on an even keel until the next tide, when she floated off without damage.

Between the wars Campbells acquired several ships, but had none built until after the Second World War when the *Bristol Queen* and *Cardiff Queen* were ordered.

These were the last two paddle steamers to join the fleet and were built on modern lines, with concealed paddle-boxes, cruiser stern and twin cowl-topped funnels.

The engines were triple-expansion with oil-fired, double-ended boilers. The activities of the Bristol firm extended well beyond the Channel, including excursions to Lundy Island and Penzance, with services operating from Torquay. But it was in 1888, the year that the Campbells moved south, that the first paddle steamer started running excursions from Torquay.

The paddle steamer *Prince* was advertised as having a landing apparatus which would allow passengers to disembark directly onto the beach, instead of being taken ashore by boat. It was the practice to run excursions to several of the steeply shelving beaches on the South Devon Coast. Slapton Sands, Bridport, Seaton, Budleigh Salterton and Lulworth Cove were all visited in this manner whereby the bows of the ship were grounded on the beach and the ship held in position with a stern anchor.

The bows were slightly cut away and strengthened to prevent damage to the hull. Passengers went ashore via a long platform which was lowered over the side of the bows. It was a hazardous method, both for the passengers and ship, and completely impossible if the water was not dead calm. In 1934 the paddle steamer *Duchess of Devonshire* met her end while attempting to carry out this type of landing at Sidmouth. The stern anchor rope parted and the ship was washed broadside on to the beach.

The *Prince* was owned by Ellett and Mathews, who, in 1892, founded the Devon Steamship Company. The *Duchess of Devonshire* was their first new ship, and four years later a slightly larger vessel, the *Duke of Devonshire,* was added. Both were built of steel and had compound diagonal engines.

There were several fleets of small paddle steamers operating from Plymouth, mainly on services on the River Tamar.

Sea trips to Dartmouth, Torquay, Salcombe and Kingsbridge were operated by the Plymouth Pier, Pavilion and Steamboat Company's *Bangor Castle* and *Princess Royal*. The manager of the Company was W. Dusting, and he ventured on an ambitious project in 1895. A separate company, the Plymouth Belle Steamship Company, was formed with one ship, the *Plymouth Belle*. Every Saturday

131

she left Penzance, calling at Falmouth, Plymouth and Torquay. She then proceeded to Guernsey where she stayed overnight. On the Sunday she went on to Jersey, made a trip around the island or to St. Malo on the French coast, and returned to Guernsey in the evening. On the Monday she returned to Torquay and then back to Penzance with stops as before. Obviously such a journey required a very seaworthy vessel, and the *Plymouth Belle* was just that. 220.5ft in length with a beam of 26.3ft she was powered by compound diagonal engines of 232 n.h.p. The promenade deck ran the full length of the ship and there were saloons fore and aft.

Unfortunately Mr. Dusting's optimism was not well founded and in 1896 the *Plymouth Belle* was on charter service at Newhaven.

In 1914 steamer services on the South Devon Coast ceased, and the paddlers went to war. Minesweeping, of course, was their major activity and many of them found themselves in strange waters, in particular the tiny *Duke of Devonshire* which steamed to Mesapotamia and back.

Both the *Duke* and *Duchess of Devonshire* emerged unscathed from the war and were back in peacetime service in 1920. They were unchallenged until 1942 when the Weymouth firm of Cosens and Co. put their paddle steamer, the *Alexandra,* into Torquay to compete against the Devon steamers. The competition lasted three seasons and then Cosens withdrew their ship and returned her to their Weymouth base.

By 1930 the effect of private motoring and motor coach tours had begun to tell, and the *Duchess of Devonshire* was withdrawn and laid up, but two years later a new threat faced the Devon Dock, Pier and Steamship Company when P & A Campbell placed the *Westward Ho!* on the South Devon Coast.

With the exception of the *Plymouth Belle* the *Westward*

132

Ho! was by far the best steamer that had plied in that area up to that time. She ran from Torquay and Plymouth, and steamed as far as Penzance with calls at Fowey, Mevagissey and Falmouth. Although the *Westward Ho!* was unable to operate services to the open beaches the *Duke of Devonshire* could not compete profitably against the Campbell ship, and she was sold to P & A Campbell in 1933. At the same time the Devon Dock, Pier and Steamship Company sold the laid-up *Duchess of Devonshire* to the South Devon and West Bay Steamship Company, and retired from the steamer excursion business.

Campbells continued with the *Westward Ho!* for one season and then withdrew, whereupon the South Devon and West Bay Steamship Company put the *Duchess of Devonshire* back at Torquay from where she operated until her unfortunate end as described earlier. After the loss of the *Duchess of Devonshire* there were no excursion paddle steamers in the area until 1936, when the *Duke of Devonshire* returned, now under the ownership of Alexander Taylor. Taylor enjoyed two successful seasons in Torquay, and it came as a surprise when he decided to pack up in 1938. Perhaps he foresaw the approach of the Second War, with the possible requisitioning of his ship, but in 1938 and 1939 there were again no paddle steamers at Torquay.

In the post-war period Torquay became the centre for pleasure steamer excursions to a greater extent than ever before.

The South Western Steam Navigation Company purchased the paddle steamer *Essex Queen* (ex *Walton Belle*) from the New Medway Steam Packet Company and renamed her *Pride of Devon*. She ran trips to Dartmouth and Start Point, but could not land on the beaches.

The days of the paddle steamer, however, were numbered. Motor vessels were becoming increasingly popular, and there were plenty of ex-naval M.V.s available which could be easily converted to pleasure cruisers. The *Pride of Devon* was broken up in 1951, and it looked as though there would be no more paddle steamers on the Devon Coast. Surprisingly, after an interval of nearly ten years, another paddler, the *Princess Elizabeth,* was purchased by Torbay Steamers and ran from Torquay for two years. Her service there was cut short because of a dispute between the owners and the Torquay Corporation, who cut off her oil supplies. This was a minor incident in the life of a ship which has a glorious war record and now lives in honourable retirement, as we shall see in Chapter 17.

We now come to some of the most delightful paddle steamers ever built. Delightful because they operated on a waterway unsurpassed in natural beauty, the River Dart. Delightful also because of their charm and elegance. They were diminutive vessels, none were longer than 108ft, with engines that gave them a top speed of about 8 knots. Quite fast enough for the type of work which they were required to do.

The first fleet of paddle steamers on the Dart was owned by the Dartmouth Steam Packet Company founded in 1859. They built up a fleet of four paddlers, starting with the *Pilot,* a wooden paddle tug with a single cylinder 'grasshopper' engine. The vessel had been built at South Shields in 1852 and plied on the Dart until 1881 when she was scrapped. An iron paddler from the yards of J. Scott Russell of Millwall, the *Dartmouth*, followed in 1871. She had two-cylinder oscillating engines, supplied by the builder.

When the Great Western Railway extended its line to Kingswear in 1864 the Dartmouth Steam Packet Company won the contract for a ferry service between Kingswear and Dartmouth. For this service they acquired the *Newcomen* which was succeeded in 1869 by the *Dolphin.*

In 1877 the Company was wound up and the four vessels were sold to a group headed by James Tolman of Dartmouth. Tolman operated the fleet on river excursions, with occasional local towage work, and in 1880 the Company ordered a new vessel specifically designed for use on the River Dart.

She was the *Berry Castle,* and was the first of a line of Dart steamers all based on the same design, and having 'Castle' in their nomenclature. Her dimensions were 108ft by 14.1ft, engines were two-cylinder oscillating driving fixed-float paddle-wheels. There were open well decks fore and aft, and a small promenade deck above the saloon.

The single, slightly raked funnel was set between the paddle-boxes, and a small bridge platform was placed immediately in front of the funnel.

Five more 'Castle' steamers were added to the fleet between 1885 and 1914. They were: the *Dartmouth Castle I* (1888), *Totnes Castle I* (1894), *Kingswear Castle I* (1904), *Dartmouth Castle II* (1907) and the *Compton Castle* (1914). In 1907 the Company changed their name to the River Dart Steamboat Company. Ships of such small dimensions were quite unsuitable for minesweeping, and the Admiralty apparently could not find any other use for them in the First World War, so they were laid up for the duration.

The post-war years saw the introduction of two small motor vessels, but the manoeuvring advantages of paddle propulsion on larger vessels was still important on the narrow, twisting river.

Consequently the paddle steamer *Totnes Castle II* was purchased in 1923, followed by the *Kingswear Castle II* in 1924. They were built to the same dimensions as the *Compton Castle* and both had two-cylinder compound diagonal engines. In company with the *Dartmouth Castle* these steamers operated the excursion service between

Dartmouth and Totnes until World War II. During the war period three of the steamers were used in a number of ways.

The *Compton Castle* became an ammunition-carrier on the Dart. The *Totnes Castle* was used as a 'liberty boat' at Plymouth, and the *Kingswear Castle* served as a Naval stores at Dittisham. The *Dartmouth Castle* was now 32 years old and she was laid up for the duration, during which time she deteriorated badly. After the war the Company converted her to a landing stage at their Millcreek yard.

The task of refitting the three remaining paddlers after the war proved to be expensive, and the *Compton Castle* and *Totnes Castle* were withdrawn in 1964, leaving the *Kingswear Castle* as the only paddle steamer on the River Dart. The fortunes of three steamers from that time are interesting, for two of them number among the handful of paddle steamers still in existence.

The *Totnes Castle* was converted into a floating 'hotel' accommodating 38 people. As can be imagined this involved considerable structural alterations, including the addition of a superstructure which completely destroyed the character of the vessel. Two years later she was sold and on November 9th, 1967, she sank off Burgh Island while being towed to Plymouth.

The *Compton Castle* was sold to Messrs. Baume and Woods of Kingsbridge who carried out extensive restoration work and moored the vessel alongside the corporation car park at Kingsbridge.

There she has remained ever since and is open to the public as a tea-shop and museum. It is interesting to note that her engines are still in working order.

The *Kingswear Castle* continued to operate until 1965 and was withdrawn at the end of that season. In 1967 she became the property of the Paddle Steamer Preservation Society who hope to maintain her in full running order.

The story of the West Country paddle steamers has been one of heartbreaks and trimphs, a continuous battle for supremacy in which Goliath always defeated David. Many fine ships plied the waters of the Bristol Channel and the Western Coast, and now they have all gone. Perhaps it is fitting that those that survived belonged to a company who went about their business unconcerned and untouched by the fight for survival that raged around them.

Chapter Thirteen

SOUTH COAST PADDLE STEAMERS

Captain Cosens of Weymouth — The Southampton Company —
Bournemouth steamers — The Sussex coast — Campbells move
to Southampton — The three-cornered battle — Campbells
defeated — Cosens and Southampton Company co-operate —
Isle of Wight Ferries — Post-war decline.

THE South Coast, for the purposes of this chapter, takes
in the counties of Sussex, Hampshire and Dorset. Three
counties which include some of the most popular holiday
resorts in England, and where paddle steamers once plied
between the piers in an almost constant stream during the
summer months.

Apart from the ferry services to the Isle of Wight the
steamers on the south coast were always pleasure excursion
vessels. It was the Victorians who discovered the delights
of going down to the sea, and it was during this period
that the popularity of the paddle steamer reached its
heyday. A steamer service from Southampton to Cowes
was operating in 1823, with the *Prince Coburg* making
twice-daily trips. A 'round the Island' excursion service
commenced in 1835 with the Portsmouth and Ryde Steam
Packet Company's *Lord Yarborough.*

From the Dorset resort of Weymouth a small steamer,
the *Rose,* ran excursions to Lyme and Southampton in
1845. She was owned by Captain Cosens and was the
forerunner of one of the major fleets to operate on the
South Coast.

Captain Cosens acquired two more vessels before he

encountered opposition in1852 from a Weymouth solicitor, Mr. Tizard, who had two steamers in operation. One of them, the *Premier,* had been built in 1846, and she was not broken up until 1937, at which time she had the distinction of being the oldest passenger ship in the world still in service.

Cosens retaliated by adding two more steamers to his fleet, the *Contractor* and the *Ocean Bride.* The competition lasted for only a few years and then Cosens and Tizard amalgamated to form the Weymouth, Bournemouth and Swanage Steam Packet Company. In 1861 there was founded the company which had the longest title in the world. The Southampton, Isle of Wight and South of England Royal Mail Steam Packet Company Limited.

The Company later became known, and still is known today, as Red Funnel Steamers, but in this chapter it will henceforth be referred to as the Southampton Co.

With two major companies based only 50 miles apart and covering the same area, it was inevitable that the competition would be fierce. The Southampton Co. started with a fleet of seven paddle steamers, to which they added at regular intervals. Cosens and Tizard kept the pace going by enlarging their fleet at about the same rate, and by 1898 things were really beginning to warm up. During this time a number of small concerns sprang up along the coast and one of them, the Bournemouth and South Coast Steam Packets, managed to survive for many years. Further along the coast, at Brighton and Hastings, the excursion business had hardly got going, the first steamer operating from Brighton being the *Brighton* in 1878, and at Hastings the *Carrick Castle* in 1885.

Both of these vessels were the nucleus of the two major companies on the Sussex Coast, the Brighton, Worthing and South Coast Steamboat Company and the Hastings, St. Leonards and Eastbourne Steamboat Company.

Returning to the Hampshire-Dorset area, the rivalry between Cosens and the Southampton Co. took a new turn in 1898 when both firms were faced with a new rival. P & A Campbell decided to set up an office in Southampton with the express purpose of operating paddle steamers in the South Coast territory. They put two of their fastest ships into the area, the *Cambria* and the *Glen Rosa*. Up until that time the paddle steamers of Cosens and the Southampton Co. had been nothing to shout about. They were slow and uncomfortable, and compared unfavourably with similar vessels in other parts of the country. The Campbell ships were both capable of 20 knots and had luxurious passenger facilities.

As it happened, however, the Southampton Co. had acquired the *Lorna Doone* in that year, a ship that had slipped through the fingers of P & A Campbell when they took over the fleet of John Gunn. Possibly the Southampton Co. foresaw the coming of Campbell's attack on their territory, but whatever their reason the acquisition of the *Lorna Doone* was to have a marked effect on the ensuing battle.

P & A Campbell opened their office in Southampton at 71 High Street, and immediately put the *Cambria* on a service which included Bournemouth, Southsea, Ryde and Sandown. *Glen Rosa* worked on the shorter trips, mainly from Southsea. The Southampton Co. ran the *Lorna Doone* as far westward as Weymouth, and eastward to Brighton. Their second ship, the *Solent Queen,* made trips to Bournemouth and the *Prince of Wales* looked after the shorter runs to Southsea and the Isle of Wight.

At Bournemouth the impact of the Campbells' arrival had yet to be felt and the Bournemouth Co. were still operating in rivalry with Cosens. The *Monarch* was Cosens' largest vessel at the time, and she was used on a variety of trips, including all-day visits to France and the Channel Islands. The Bournemouth Co.'s *Brodick Castle* made trips to Torquay and Dartmouth. In 1899 the two companies agreed to share the Bournemouth-Swanage service, Cosens using the *Empress* and the Bournemouth Co. the *Lord Elgin*.

The *Glen Rosa* ran only for the 1898 season, and in 1899 the *Cambria* was the sole Campbell ship on the South Coast. But this did not mean that the Campbells had lost interest, for in 1900 they brought the *Albion* to Southampton. The *Albion* had run for one season in the Bristol Channel under her original name of *Slieve Donard*. She had been built in 1893 for the Belfast, County Down Railway Company, from whom she was purchased by Campbells.

The main danger to the Southampton Co.'s trade, however, was still the *Cambria,* and despite extensive refits the *Lorna Doone* was no match for her rival. In order to regain their supremacy the Company ordered a new, fast steamer which came into service in July 1900. The new ship was the *Balmoral,* built by S. McKnight and Co. of Ayr. The *Balmoral* was 236ft long by 27.1ft. beam, with a promenade deck extending the full length and width of the hull. There was a spacious aft saloon on the main deck and a dining saloon below. A set of two-cylinder compound diagonal engines of 300 n.h.p. supplied the power, the diameter of the high pressure cylinder being 36.5 inches and the low pressure 66.5 inches. The stroke was 66 inches. Her speed of 20 knots was about the same as that of the *Cambria* and as both ships were used on day trips to Cherbourg the rivalry quickly developed into a series of races.

Considerable public interest was aroused by the competition and crowds would gather on Bournemouth Pier in the evening to see the two contestants as they raced for home.

On most occasions there was no more than a ship's length between them, and often a dead-heat resulted.

Some idea of the speed of these vessels can be gained by the scheduled departure and arrival times. The *Cambria* departed from Southampton at 8.00 a.m., calling at Bournemouth at 10 a.m., and arrived at Cherbourg at 1.30 p.m. The return trip commenced at 4.30 p.m. and the arrival time at Bournemouth was 8.15 p.m. On one occasion the *Balmoral* did the return trip in 3 hours 37 minutes at an average speed of 18 knots.

While the competition between P & A Campbell and the Southampton Co. was now fairly evenly matched, the effect on both Cosens and the Bournemouth Co. was rather drastic. Neither of them could hope to compete against the *Cambria* and the *Balmoral* on the cross-channel runs, and on the shorter routes they were outclassed by the *Lorna Doone* and the *Albion*.

In 1901 Cosens took the bold step of purchasing a new steamer, the *Majestic*. It was a bold step because the *Majestic* was actually smaller and slower than the Campbell ships, but she had the advantage of possessing triple-expansion engines. This type of engine was very smooth running, and Cosens banked on the appeal that this would have to passengers who preferred a restful journey to the swaying, vibrating motion that was characteristic of ships with big compound diagonals.

The *Majestic*'s dimensions were 215.5ft in length with a 27.1ft beam. The engines had three diagonal cylinders of 21 inches, 35 inches and 54 inches diameter respectively. The stroke was 60 inches and the power derived was 226 n.h.p.

Cosens' gamble was fully justified and the *Majestic* served her owners well until the First World War. Regrettably she was sunk while minesweeping in the Mediterranean.

Bournemouth Pier was the centre of much paddle steamer activity in 1901 and 1902. Cosens and the Bournemouth Co. continued their co-operation on the

Swanage service, and Cosens brought the *Brodick Castle* from the Bournemouth Co. who were now left with only the *Lord Elgin*. Trips to France and the Channel Islands were run by the larger ships of the three major companies, and there was a variety of coastal trips to Torquay, Swanage, Lulworth Cove and the Isle of Wight. So intense was the traffic that, on May 10th, 1901, the *Albion* collided with the *Empress* while both vessels were backing out from Bournemouth Pier.

In the Southampton area the local company purchased their first steel-built paddler, the *Queen,* in time for the Whitsun Holiday of 1902. She was used on the Cowes service and also was a frequent visitor to Bournemouth.

1902 was the year of the Coronation of King Edward VII, and part of the celebrations was a Naval Review at Spithead.

This tremendous attraction drew steamers from all parts of the South Coast and beyond. Three of the 'Belle' steamers, *Walton Belle, Yarmouth Belle* and *Southwold Belle,* arrived from London. The Torquay steamers, *Duke of Devonshire* and *Duchess of Devonshire* were there, and Campbells brought the *Princess May* round from the Bristol Channel.

A few days before Coronation Day the King was taken ill and the whole proceedings were postponed. The Fleet, however, had already assembled at Spithead and provided good business for the pleasure steamer operators, many of them temporarily abandoning their regular services to meet the demand.

Two months later the Coronation took place, and the Fleet, which had dispersed in the meantime, re-assembled. The Naval Review was held on August 16th, 1902, providing a double bonus for the excursion organisers.

Prior to the commencement of the 1902 season P & A Campbell had spread their influence further by the take-over of the Brighton, Worthing and South Coast

143

Company. They now had vessels operating from all the major resorts on the South Coast, and it looked as though the scene was set for the elimination of all their rivals, as had happened elsewhere. But this time the local 'Davids' were too strong for Goliath. At the end of the 1902 season P & A Campbell withdrew from Southampton and Bournemouth. Possibly they had underestimated the strength of the opposition. Obviously it was a mistake to take on three companies at once, and while there was never any attempt by Cosens, the Southampton Co. and Bournemouth Co. to close their ranks against the invader, local loyalties were strong and must have affected the final outcome of the struggle.

If they had achieved nothing else the intervention of the Bristol firm had raised the standard of paddle steamers on the South Coast. With Campbells out of the way, the Bournemouth Co. and Cosens continued to work together, and the Southampton Co. to compete against them. The *Balmoral* now made her Cherbourg trips with only the slower *Majestic* as a rival, the *Lorna Doone* began to attack the Bournemouth trade, and the *Lord Elgin* served the Bournemouth-Swanage route as before.

In the Sussex area Campbells were still operating with the *Brighton Queen*. This paddle steamer was one of the most popular on the South Coast. She had been purchased by the Brighton & Worthing Co. to compete against the *Plymouth Belle,* when that ship was on charter at Newhaven. The *Brighton Queen* was built by the Clydebank Shipbuilding and Engineering Company, forerunners of John Brown and Company.

Her length was 240.5ft, beam 28.1ft and her gross tonnage was 603. Her engines were two-cylinder compound diagonal. The promenade deck ran the full length of the hull and there were saloons fore and aft on the main deck. Before the 1903 season she was modified to improve her accommodation, and her speed was raised from 18¼ knots to 19½ knots. During the season she was joined by the *Glen Rosa,* and these two ships were Campbells principal steamers on the Sussex Coast for several years. They were supplemented from time to time by other steamers brought round from Bristol; the *Waverley, Ravenswood* and the *Bonnie Doon* were all used in the Brighton area for the period between 1902 and 1914, and in 1913 the *Glen Rosa* was replaced by the *Albion.*

The day after the declaration of the Great War, August 5th, 1914, the *Brighton Queen* was scheduled to sail to Boulogne.

The trip was cancelled, and a few days later the ship was taken to Bristol to lie up. Eventually she was taken over by the Admiralty, and sank off the Belgian coast, in 1915, after striking a mine.

On the Bournemouth station further additions were made to the fleet in 1908, two by the Southampton Co. and one by Cosens. The new steamer announced by Cosens was the *Emperor of India,* but she was in fact a ship which had been rejected by the Southampton Co. in 1906. Originally named *Princess Royal,* she had failed to meet her contractual requirements and the Southampton Co. had returned her to the builders, J. Thorneycroft and Sons. Considerable modifications were carried out which included lengthening the hull to increase the buoyancy.

The Southampton Co.'s new ships were the *Stirling Castle* and the *Bournemouth Queen.* The *Stirling Castle* was placed on the Swanage service in April 1908, but in July she was replaced by the *Bournemouth Queen,* who worked from Bournemouth for the next 33 years.

The friendly co-operation that had existed between Cosens and the Bournemouth Co. ended abruptly in 1909 when the latter sold the *Lord Elgin,* their only ship, to the Southampton Co., along with the goodwill of the business. There was no question of co-operation between Cosens and the Southampton Co., quite the opposite in fact, for the *Lord Elgin* was now supported on the Swanage service by the *Stirling Castle*. Cosens was forced to put the *Monarch* on this service with the *Brodick Castle* to compete against the Southampton vessels, so that there were now four steamers on this run regardless of the traffic requirements.

With the competition now reduced to a straight fight, the Southampton Co. made a determined bid to gain the monopoly at Bournemouth. But Cosens held on grimly, the popularity of the paddle steamers was still at its height and there was plenty of trade to keep both companies going.

At one time the Southampton Co. even attempted to compete against Cosens on the Lulworth Cove excursions. The *Lord Elgin* and the *Stirling Castle* were scheduled to make these trips, and landing was to be by small boats. As it happened the weather intervened and the trips were never made.

In 1911 the Southampton Co. made some changes, one being the removal of the *Lord Elgin* from Bournemouth. She was replaced by the *Princess Helena*. The *Lord Elgin* ran for a short while on the Southampton, Cowes and Portsmouth packet service, but she was soon replaced by a new ship, the *Princess Mary*. As it happened the *Lord Elgin* outlived her successor by many years. The *Princess Mary,* on the other hand, became a war casualty, although not during the war. It was after the Armistice had been signed that she struck the submerged wreck of H.M.S. *Majestic,* a battleship that had been sunk in the Dardenelles.

At the end of 1909 season the faithful old *Brodick Castle* had become redundant as a result of the acquisition of the *Emperor of India*. Cosens sold her to a South American firm as a cattle-boat, and, stripped of all her fittings, engines, boilers, funnels and passenger accommodation, she left Weymouth under tow. She did not get very far, for as soon as she was out of Weymouth Bay she sank.

Cosens put five steamers into service between 1911 and 1914, two of which were chartered. The last one, acquired in 1913, was the *Alexandra,* the ship that later became the *Showboat* described in Chapter Four.

Steamer excursions continued until the end of the season in 1914, except for the cross-channel trips which were stopped as soon as the war was declared. The story of the work of the paddle steamers during the war will be told in another chapter, but before picking up the story of the South Coast paddlers after the war there is one service which has not been mentioned so far.

Steamer services to the Isle of Wight took on a new importance with the coming of the railways, and before the railway companies ran their own fleets there were two concerns operating in conjunction with the railway service to Portsmouth. The earliest one, the Port of Portsmouth and Ryde Steam Packet Company commenced in 1850 with three vessels, *Her Majesty, Princess Royal* and *Prince of Wales.* In 1873 the Southsea and Isle of Wight Steam Ferry Company were formed and they had a fleet of four screw steamers. The two companies combined in 1876 to form the Port of Portsmouth and Ryde United Steam Packet Company, and in 1850 the London and South West, and London, Brighton and South Coast Railways took over the concern, which then became known as the Joint Railways fleet.

Steamer services to the Island between Lymington and Yarmouth were started in 1850 by the Solent Steamship Company with a single paddle steamer, the *Solent.*

The London and South West Railway took them over in 1884.

At the beginning of the first war, Cosens had eleven steamers, the Southampton Co. thirteen, Joint Railways six and P & A Campbell, on the South coast, had three. When hostilities ceased Cosens had lost one ship, the Southampton Co. two, Joint Railways one and P & A Campbell one.

Services re-started slowly after the war as the ships were returned from wartime duties. The *Balmoral* now ran alone on the cross-channel trips, Cosens having lost the *Majestic*. The Swanage service was down to two ships once more, the *Stirling Castle* and *Princess Mary* being the Southampton Co.'s losses. At Brighton P & A Campbell were without a fleet until 1923, for not only had they lost the *Brighton Queen* but in addition the *Glen Rosa* and the *Albion* were unfit for further service and had to be scrapped.

A paddle steamer, the *Lady Rowena,* ran from Brighton in 1921 under the ownership of a Mr. F. C. Deering, and in 1922 two new companies were formed. One of these, the Channel Excursions Steamers Ltd., purchased one of the 'Belle' steamers, *Woolwich Belle,* and renamed her *Queen of the South*. The other company, the Cinque Ports Steam Navigation Company, did not own any steamers, but ran the *Emperor of India* on charter from Cosens.

When Campbells started up again they did so with *Devonia*. She was later joined by the *Lady Evelyn* which was renamed *Brighton Belle*. Later in the season the *Ravenswood* was brought round from Bristol. This kind of opposition was too much for the two companies which had started in the previous year, and the *Emperor of India* went back to Bournemouth while the *Queen of the South* was sold to the New Medway Steam Packet Company.

In 1923, the Southern Railway Company became successors to the two companies operating railway steamers and in 1924 they commenced replacing their fleet. The *Shanklin* replaced the *Duchess of Richmond,* which had been lost during the war, and four years later the *Portsdown* and *Merstone* took over from the *Duchess of Albany* and the *Princess Margaret,* which were sold

148

for scrap. During 1930 two new steamers, the *Southsea* and the *Whippingham,* were introduced for excursion work to Brighton and Bournemouth, and for Round the Island trips. In 1934 the *Sandown* replaced the *Duchess of Kent.* The Company's final acquisition before the second war was the *Ryde,* in 1937, and she was the last paddle steamer to be built for service anywhere on the South Coast.

As the war years faded, Cosens and the Southampton Co. continued to compete against each other at Bournemouth.

But the heyday of the paddle steamers was over, the rivalry was less intense than in pre-war days and by 1930 a 'live and let live' policy existed between the two companies. Tickets were made interchangeable, and services were put on an alternate day basis, so that the two companies never actually competed against each other. Additions and replacements to the fleets were made less frequently than of old. The Southampton Co. took delivery of a new steamer in 1927 for the Southampton-Cowes service. She was the *Princess Elizabeth,* named after our present Queen. In 1931 their first motor vessel went into service, but five years later they reverted to a paddle steamer which they named *Gracie Fields.* The ship was launched by the famous singer, to the strains of 'Sing as we Go'.

Cosens parted with the *Alexandra* in 1930, and in 1937 they purchased a steamer from the Southern Railway, the *Duchess of Norfolk.*

Under the name of *Embassy* she re-opened some of the pre-war all-day trips that had been the province of the *Emperor of India.* At the end of the season Cosens scrapped the *Premier,* a ship that had served for 91 years, 85 of them on the South Coast. She was replaced by the *Consul,* which was none other than the Torquay paddle steamer the *Duke of Devonshire.*

When war came again there were 28 paddle steamers on the South Coast, the biggest fleet being that of the Southampton Co. with 10. When the war ended the total had been reduced to 22. This time all the Cosens steamers survived, but Southern Railways lost two, the *Southsea* and the *Portsdown,* Campbells lost the *Brighton Queen* and *Waverley,* and the Southampton Co.'s *Gracie Fields* and *Her Majesty* failed to return.

The prospects for trade looked good in the immediate post-war years. The war-weary public were anxious to throw off the depressing mantle of five harrowing years, and the majority of the South Coast resorts made determined efforts to cater for the flood of visitors.

Cosens, not surprisingly, were the first to re-start excursion sailings, with the *Empress* and the *Victoria*. They commenced at Weymouth in June 1946, but were very quickly followed by the Southampton Co. who put the *Princess Elizabeth* on the Southampton-Ryde service in July. The Bournemouth-Swanage service re-opened later that year, Cosens using the *Monarch* and the *Embassy* and the Southampton Co. the *Princess Elizabeth*.

The Southern Railway Company, soon to be nationalised, were hard pressed to keep up with the demand for transport to the Isle of Wight, and during the summer months large queues formed on Portsmouth Harbour Station as the depleted fleet plied back and forth across the Solent. In 1948 British Railways introduced two diesel vessels, and eventually phased out all their paddle steamers, the last one being the *Ryde*.

On the Sussex coast Campbells did not get started until 1947, with the *Glen Gower,* but she was soon replaced by a turbine steamer, the *Empress Queen.*

The *Britannia* went to Brighton in 1948 and stayed for two seasons, she was now oil-fired and had two funnels. During the years 1950 and 1951 there were no paddle steamers at Brighton , but in 1952 Campbells sent one of their newest steamers to the Sussex resort. This was the *Cardiff Queen,* built in 1947 to the latest paddle steamer designs. Apart from her triple-expansion engines she had concealed paddle-boxes, a regrettable trend in design which appears to have been an attempt to give the impression that the vessel was screw-driven. Indeed, from a distance it was difficult to tell the difference, the only clue being the broad wake spreading outward from the paddle-wheels. The *Cardiff Queen* did not return for the 1953 season, instead, the *Glen Gower* operated there until 1956 and was used in that, and the previous year, on 'no-passport' trips to France.

But now the days of the paddle steamer were rapidly coming to an end, not only on the South Coast but in all parts of the country.

The *Glen Gower* worked the 1957 season in the Bristol Channel and was then laid up. When she was scrapped two years later the oldest set of paddle engines in Britain went with her. Two other great names had already gone, the *Ravenswood* had been scrapped in October 1955 and the *Britannia* at the end of 1956. In 1960 a paddle steamer was again seen at Brighton when the *Freshwater II* was renamed *Sussex Queen* and made trips to Eastbourne, but she was not a success and in 1961 moved on to Bournemouth to become the *Swanage Queen.*

Returning to the Bournemouth scene, Cosens were making the most of their good fortune in still having an intact fleet, but the Southampton Co. were having great difficulty in supplying ships for all the areas that they normally covered. Their wartime losses had really been four, for in addition to the two that were sunk, the *Balmoral* and the *Lorna Doone* were returned completely unfit for further work and had to be scrapped.

In 1949 the Company bought two steamers from the New Medway Steam Packet Company, the *Queen of Thanet* and the *Queen of Kent,* and renamed them *Solent*

151

Queen and *Lorna Doone*. The *Solent Queen* ran from Southampton while the *Lorna Doone* relieved the *Bournemouth Queen* at Bournemouth.

By 1952, however, things were not going well for either company. The Southampton firm had suffered a serious loss in the previous year when the *Solent Queen* caught fire while undergoing repairs. The damage was so extensive that the ship was sold for breaking. Cosens scrapped the *Monarch* in 1950, and transferred the name to the *Shanklin*, which they bought from British Railways in 1951. Finally the *Lorna Doone* and *Bournemouth Queen* were moved to Southampton, leaving Cosens the sole operator at Bournemouth.

From 1952 onwards the story is one of withdrawals and scrappings, with no replacements. *Lorna Doone* went in March 1952, the *Princess Helena* in July. The 80-year-old *Lord Elgin* was scrapped in 1955, as was the *Empress*. The *Empress* had the only remaining set of oscillating engines in the world, and these are now preserved at the Maritime Museum in Southampton. The *Emperor of India* and the *Bournemouth Queen* were sold to Belgian ship breakers in 1957 and only the *Consul* and the *Embassy* managed to survive for a few years longer.

But they too were doomed, and by the end of 1967 the South Coast paddlers were no more. For over 140 years they had churned the waters of the English Channel, and with an enviable record of safety. Fog was always a hazard, for a sea mist can rise in the English Channel with frightening suddenness. Without navigational aids, such as Radar, experience and good seamanship were essential virtues in the paddle steamers' captains.

There were incidents, like the time in 1886 when the *Heather Bell* nearly became a part of the Isle of Wight as she steamed through dense fog straight for the Needles. Only the frantic shouts from a lone angler averted a terrible tragedy.

During the same period the *Queen* went on to the rocks in West Bay, and escaped undamaged. Less fortunate was the *Bournemouth* which, three days earlier, piled up on the rocks at Portland Bill and broke her back. Yet these were the only outstanding incidents in the whole history of the South Coast paddlers, and they involved no loss of life.

The piers that were built to serve these ships are still there, their landing stages now used only by anglers, and their Victorian architecture is a reminder of the period that is recognised as the paddle steamer heyday.

If one stands at the end of one of these piers, say at Brighton, Bournemouth or Swanage, all that can be seen is a lonely expanse of sea. No distant smoke on the horizon, to herald the approach of a steamer, no sound of thrashing, pounding paddle-wheels as another crowded excursion boat arrives. These sights and sounds have gone forever, and the South Coast is poorer because of it.

Chapter Fourteen

TUGS AND TUGMEN

Early paddle tugs — The art of 'seeking' — The Watkins tugs — Royal Navy padddle tugs.

FROM the beginning of the 19th century the paddle steamer made rapid strides in its development, and soon ousted the sailing ships from the inland and coastal services. On the high seas, however, the fast windjammers and clippers were in use well into the second half of the century. They ran in direct competition with the ocean paddlers, and were often superior to them when running before a favourable wind. Competition was fierce, and it was important that the advantages of a fast run should not be lost by waiting for a favourable breeze to take them into port. And so, at the end of their voyage, they came to rely upon the services of steam vessels. Not the giant paddlers that sailing ship owners and masters alike held in utter contempt, but the tiny paddle tugs. Good prices were paid for a tow, and consequently the business of towage became highly competitive, and provides one of the most colourful stories in the history of the paddle steamer.

In the early days the paddle tugs were tiny vessels of low power, often not capable of towing a ship against the tide. They were unable to venture far for fear of running out of coal, and on more than one occasion a tug had been known to borrow coal from its tow in order to keep up steam. Their work, therefore, was confined mainly to moving vessels in and out of dock, or for getting a ship far enough down river to pick up a fair wind.

The Crimean War of 1854-56 provided a boom for the Thames tugs, as the stores ships which loaded at Woolwich Arsenal and the Deptford military stores could not afford to wait for the wind and tide. The standards of the tugs improved, and although they were still powered by the extravagant jet-condenser engines they became more powerful and able to steam for greater distances. After taking their outward-bound tow down the English Channel as far as the Downs they would wait for the Australian clippers heading for London.

It was a Gravesend tug owner, Richard Ross, who started this practice, before long other companies followed suit, and the art of 'seeking' developed. Obviously the further down the Channel a tug could get, the better were the chances of picking up a profitable tow, but at the same time enough coal had to be preserved for the return trip. Sails were often used to aid the tug on its outward journey, sometimes a mizzen set abaft the funnel, or a square foresail. The bunkers would be crammed with coal, with more on deck, so that the sponsons were at water level, reducing the efficiency of the paddles.

To get the best of both worlds the tug owners tried to arrange for outward tows as well as seeking homecomers. The fast passenger-carrying windjammers would announce in their sailing advertisements that they were 'taking steam down to the Downs' or 'taking steam down Channel', 'taking steam' being the expression used for employing a tow.

The favourite area for seeking was just off the Isle of Wight. Here the tugs would gather, and it was the practice to send the Mate ashore at daybreak to climb the heights of St. Boniface Down. From this vantage point he could watch for incoming ships, and at the same time note if any rival tugs had secretly left the area overnight. So experienced were these men that they could put a name to a ship as soon as her top-royals appeared over the horizon.

The South Coast ports were useful places for obtaining information. The tug owners employed agents at these places to pick up reports of homecoming ships, which they passed on to the tug skippers. Every waterside tavern had a copy of the Shipping Gazette and the tug skippers would examine this with an expert eye. It was rather like studying the form of a horse; winds, tides, the characteristics of each ship, and of its Master, were all taken into account.

Finally the skipper would decide where a ship should be and at what time, and he was nearly always right.

The ability of some skippers became so well-known that, having made up his mind where to go, he had to make sure that no one picked his brains and followed him. The totally unlawful method of moving off at night without showing navigation lights was commonplace, and a silent steam windlass was also an advantage. Steaming with the navigation lights reversed, so that the vessel appeared to be coming instead of going, was another favourite trick.

On board the homecoming ships there was just as much keenness to pick up a good tow. Among the tugs that went seeking were some that were in a very poor condition, and these were known as 'toshers'. If a captain were unfortunate enough to be towed by one of these vessels he was liable to find himself being overtaken by a rival, and so it was with a wary eye that he viewed an offer of a tow.

Screw tugs came into use in the 1870's, but the majority of ship's masters favoured the paddlers. They could hold the water better, (a screw tug would often lift its screw clear of the water when pulling against a strong tide), and on the river they could turn a ship almost within its own length.

Although competition between the tug masters was fierce, and of a 'no holds barred' nature, once contact had been made with a possible tow the successful skipper was left in possession. The tugboat captains were free to negotiate terms with the ship's master, and these discussions were usually made easier by the delivery of fresh provisions and newspapers.

Satisfactory terms having been agreed upon the long haul would commence. Good manila rope, 12 to 16 inches in diameter, was always the favourite towline, and this was usually provided by the tow. The art of towing called for supreme skill on the part of all of the tug's crew.

In calm weather it was not too difficult, but in bad conditions, or at night, there was a danger that the tow may drift off course or overtake the tug. Many a tug had its funnel dented by the bowsprit of its tow, and on one occasion a tug had the dolphin striker of her tow driven through her deck.

The towage business developed rapidly in all of Britain's major ports and rivers, but the first steam tugs were used on the Clyde in 1819 by the Clyde Shipping Company. The Tyne soon followed suit, and it was in 1832 that the first paddle tug was seen on the Thames. This was the *Lady Dundas*, an ex-Tyne vessel, and she was followed by the *Wear* from Sunderland. The ex-owners of the *Wear* knew what they were doing when they sold her, for she was quite incapable of towing a heavy ship. This did nothing to encourage prospective tug owners to invest their money in this new type of vessel, but there were a few who could see the possibilities of towing. Among them was John Roger Watkins.

Watkins started his business in 1833, taking his younger son, William, into the firm with him. Their first vessel was the *Monarch,* a wooden built tug of 65ft in length with a 14ft beam. Her single engine developed 20 n.h.p. and steam was supplied by a flue boiler. In later years paddle tugs were built with double engines driving each paddle wheel separately. By putting one engine in reverse and one full ahead these tugs could turn sharply, but the *Monarch,* was able to achieve a similar manoeuvre by using a device invented by John Watkins. This was the 'chain box', a box on wheels filled with chain which could be run across the deck, causing one paddle wheel to dip deeper into the water and the other to lift clear.

The *Monarch*'s range was very limited, she carried only seven tons of coal, and she worked mainly from St. Katharine Dock assisting the big ships down the river. In the 1830's she worked on charter to the Royal Navy, and she is the tug depicted in Turner's famous painting 'The Fighting Temeraire'.

By 1840 the Watkins concern had prospered sufficiently to warrant the purchase of another tug. Instead of going north for the new vessel, the Watkins' placed the order locally, at Limehouse, where they could keep a watchful eye on the construction. Little is known about this second Watkins tug, except that she was called *Fiddler* and was more powerful than the *Monarch.*

Six more tugs joined the Watkins fleet during the next ten years, and then came the advent of long range seeking. Two tugs, the *Britannia* and the *Victoria,* were built for this purpose, and they soon proved to be superior to their rivals. The *Victoria* particularly was an impressive vessel. Built of oak and teak and with a gross tonnage of 152 she was the biggest and most powerful tug on the river. Ship owners began to favour the Watkins tugs and before long the firm had a virtual monopoly of long distance towing. On one occasion the *Britannia* towed the 735-ton *Columbia* from Deptford to Calais Roads, the longest tow ever tackled up to that time.

The fairly straightforward task of towing vessels down river was only one of the many jobs undertaken. At that time shipbuilding was a major industry on Thameside and

Watkins tugs took part in many launchings, including that of the *Great Eastern,* and the first iron-clad warship H.M.S. *Warrior.*

Salvage was another profitable sideline, and a lesser known but useful service was that of towing dredgers to various ports and harbours on the Continent.

These long distance tows were made possible by the introduction of the surface condenser and the use of two boilers, but fuel consumption was still a problem. In 1866 Watkins achieved a major breakthrough in paddle tug design with their famous vessel the *Anglia.* The *Anglia* had three boilers and three funnels. The funnels were set two abaft the paddle-boxes and one forward, which earned her the nickname of 'Three-fingered Jack'. She carried the largest coal bunkers ever put in a tug, which she needed for she was extravagant on fuel.

The boilers were tubular and her side-lever engines developed 700 i.h.p. making her the most powerful tug in the world. It is a tribute to her designers that, when she was ten years old, the *Anglia* was awarded first prize for tug design at the Naval Architects Exhibition. Naturally the *Anglia* was very successful on seeking work and long distance tows, but she also carried out some unusual jobs, perhaps the most unusual being the 'Cleopatra Needle' tow.

The famous obelisk, which stands on the Thames Embankment, was being transported through the Mediterranean in a steel pontoon when it broke away from the towing steamer. The *Anglia* was sent to Southern Spain, where the 'Needle' had beached, and successfully completed the operation of bringing it to London.

Experiments with screw tugs were carried out by Watkins in 1869, but it was ten years before the change-over from paddle to screw began. In the meantime an improved version of the *Anglia* was launched in 1870.

Built by the Thames Ironworks the *Cambria* was fitted

with two-cylinder side-lever engines. She was designed to undertake long journeys, and had spacious cabins which could be converted to saloons for occasional passenger work. The *Cambria* continued to operate long after the screw tugs came into use and survived until 1913. When she went to the breakers' yard only the *Iona*, bought by Watkins in 1886, remained as the last paddle tug on the Thames.

As the screw tugs improved in design, power and economy the paddle tugs began to lose favour. But for many years the two types worked side by side, particularly in the Royal Navy. The manoeuvrability of the paddle tugs in the crowded waters of naval dockyards was a big advantage and the Admiralty built many fine vessels of this type, including diesel-electric tugs some of which are still in use today. Their largest steam paddle tug was the *Pert,* built in 1916. The *Pert* was 178ft long and was fitted with compound diagonal engines of 2,000 i.h.p. driving 14ft diameter paddle wheels.

She was reputed to be able to tow three destroyers at one time.

Generally speaking, however, the paddle tugs had given way to the screw in the larger ports and harbours by the 1920's. Only in the North East, where the tugboat was born, were they still in use until the 1960's, mainly because coal was cheap in that area. Nowadays the tugboat is a powerful rugged diesel-driven vessel fitted with wireless, radar and all the other benefits of modern marine technology. But they still bear the lines of their illustrious ancestors, the squat hull, broad beam and blunt bow makes them instantly recognisable. Today tug skippers are far removed from their rough, tough, often illiterate predecessors. But one thing they have in common, that special skill which makes a tug-master different from any other mariner, in the same way that the tugboat is different from any other vessel.

Chapter Fifteen

RIVERBOATS OF AMERICA
AND AUSTRALIA

The Hudson River — Great Lakes steamers — Mississippi steamboats — The race between the *Natchez* and *Robert E. Lee* —
The Delaware River — Australia's 'Mississippi' — The Murray
River boats — Cadell and Randell compete — Riverboat
skippers — The *Coonawarra*.

OF all the paddle steamers that plied the rivers of the
world none can match the glamour, romance and fame
of the American riverboats. They have been immortalised
in song, on the stage and screen and in the works of some
of America's greatest authors. They were as much a part
of that nation as the stagecoach and the covered wagon,
for long before the coming of the railroad the steamboats
were helping to open up the unknown territories of a
continent.

As we have seen in Chapter One, Robert Fulton was
the man who first made the paddle steamer a commercial
success. We have also seen that he destroyed all prospects
of development by competition on the Hudson River when
he gained the monopoly of the river trade.

Not that Fulton's *Clermont* was an instant success, it
was greeted with mixed feeling ranging from distrust on
the part of the passengers to downright terror by the
Hudson Valley farmers, who feared that their crops would
be ruined by this smoke-belching monster. Once these
fears had been allayed, however, the steamboat idea
spread to other areas. The Ohio River, Lake Champlain,
The Great Lakes, Long Island Sound, all had steamboats

11   161

operating within a few years of Fulton's venture, and it was in these areas that the American paddle steamers began to develop and improve.

The Ohio Indians called them 'Walk-in-the-Water' and a steamboat of that name was one of the first to trade on Lake Erie. She was built by the famous New York shipbuilder, Noah Brown, at Black Rock, now called Buffalo. She was the first steamer to be built above the falls of Niagara, and although she could steam from Buffalo to Detroit in 44 hours, her return journey had to be partly assisted by a team of oxen towing her against the current of the Niagara River.

The *Walk-in-the-Water* plied this route for three years, carrying supplies to the settlers and returning with skins and furs. In 1821 she was caught in a furious gale and foundered on the rocks near Buffalo, her engine was later used in the *Superior*. Another product of Noah Brown, the *Superior* was built with a deep-water hull, a design which became adopted by most of the Great Lake steamers.

Fulton, and his partner Robert Livingston, held the monopoly on the Hudson until 1824. Several attempts were made to set up in opposition to the Fulton-Livingston concern, but none succeeded, and in 1824 there were fewer steamboats operating on the Hudson than on any other comparable waterway in America. The *Clermont* was joined by the *Car of Neptune, Paragon* and *Firefly,* and was eventually replaced by the *Richmond*. The *Chancellor Livingston* was built at the yards of Henry Eckford, but Fulton did not live to see her launched.

He died in 1815, and nine years later his monopoly was broken forever by a decision of the United States Supreme Court.

The declaration that the Hudson River was a Federal waterway started a boom in the shipbuilding industry. Steamboat companies sprang up almost overnight and within a few years there were five major lines operating on the river. The competition led, of course, to racing, often with disastrous results. A number of steamboat 'Barons' emerged during this period, men like 'Uncle Dan'l Drew', 'Live Oak' George Law, and the Vander-bilts, who thought nothing of deliberately ramming an opponent. The struggle only abated when the steamboats became threatened by the railroad, and some, like the Vanderbilts, decided to exploit this new means of trans-portation. But for many years there was enough business to keep the railroads and the steamboats fully occupied. Large and luxurious boats were designed, capable of carrying a good payload of freight and passengers.

Many had the facilities of first-class hotels; spacious lounges and saloons with an orchestra to provide enter-tainment. The boom lasted well into the 1900's, until the coming of the automobile and the truck.

The *Clermont* had only been in operation for two years when Fulton and Livingston began to look around for fresh fields to conquer. And the complex system of the Mississippi, with its many tributaries, was an obvious choice. They found that there were about 7,000 miles of navigable water, and not only was there an abundance of wood for fuel but, in Ohio, a good supply of coal. A steamboat was built at Pittsburgh, Pennsylvania, and named *New Orleans*. She was 100ft long and had side paddle-wheels driven by a low pressure engine of Fulton's design. In September 1811, her pilot, Andy Jack, carefully eased his charge out of the quiet waters of the Monogahela River into the fast-flowing current of the Ohio, and set course for New Orleans, 2,000 miles away.

The journey must rate as one of the most eventful ever undertaken by a paddle steamer anywhere in the world. After negotiating the falls of Ohio, no mean feat in itself, the *New Orleans* steamed southward. But before she had gone very far the most dreaded of nature's phenomenoms took a hand. The earthquake of 1811 began.

For days the earth trembled. The river flooded, and the banks crumbled and were swept away. The *New Orleans* was battered by floating debris, fire broke out on board, and hostile Indians, convinced that the vessel was the cause of the upheaval, pursued her in their war canoes. But she steamed gallantly on, and at last reached the lower river, to become the first steamboat on the Mississippi. Fulton and Livingston immediately set out to monopolise the river trade as they had done on the Hudson. But in a test case against Captain Henry M. Shreve they were beaten.

Shreve, a river-man from boyhood, designed steamboats which set the unmistakable style of the Mississippi paddlers. They had broad, shallow-draught hulls, with the engines placed on the main deck. Stern wheels, which could be raised, were used on vessels plying on the upper rivers, particularly the Missouri. Above the main deck were either one or two enclosed decks standing on stilt-like wooden supports. The crew were quartered in a long, narrow cabin, called a 'texas', which was placed on the top deck and above this sat the tiny wheelhouse. The engines were usually high pressure and were fed by tubular boilers. Above all this towered the two slender funnels with their ornate 'crowns'.

Travelling on the river in those days was a hazardous business. In most places the river was extremely shallow, and even the most experienced river-pilots were hard put to keep up with the ever-changing currents and channels.

Snags were a constant danger, these were broken tree-trunks projecting from the mud, with a jagged end lying just under the surface, capable of ripping open the hull of a vessel. Tornadoes and cyclones added further dangers and the boats themselves were prone to catching fire, their wooden construction and cargoes of cotton bales being a tinder-dry match for any stray spark.

Fig. 17 — One of the great Mississipi steamboat races, the NATCHEZ versus the ECLIPSE.
(Photo Science Museum, London).

Fig. 18—H.M.S. TERRIBLE. One of the most powerful steam warships
of her time.   (Photo Science Museum, London).

Fig. 19 — H.M.S. GORGON. First of the paddle frigates. Carried
two 10 inch guns and four thirty-pounders.
                              (Photo Science Museum, London).

If the traveller managed to survive all the possible mishaps that could befall the vessel he was still in danger from that most famous of Mississippi characters, the professional gambler. The gamblers lived on the river-boats, and despite warning notices many an unsuspecting cotton merchant was cleaned out in a game of Poker, or was shot by a quickly-drawn Derringer if he dared to question his opponent's honesty.

The steamboat trade developed so rapidly that by 1834 the Mississippi tonnage exceeded that of Britain. There were 231 boats on the river at that time, and fifteen years later the figure was 958.

The Civil War divided the riverboats into the rival camps, and the Mississippi became a vital highway in the pursuance of war. Some vessels were used to transport soldiers and supplies, others were hastily converted to gunboats and took part in major engagements such as the battle of Memphis and Vicksburgh.

The Battle of Memphis took place on June 6th, 1862. Steamboats of the Union and Confederancy met and slogged it out at point-blank range. The Union victory placed Memphis in Northern hands and led to another fierce battle at Vicksburgh. The converted riverboats had their lower decks protected by cotton bales and railroad iron, while the pilot took shelter behind sheets of iron.

But both sides also constructed iron-clad rams, such as the *Lafayette* and the *Merrimac*. Although heavily armoured these vessels were vulnerable to concentrated fire aimed at the paddle-boxes, and once the paddles were out of action they became sitting ducks, to be finished off at leisure.

After the war riverboats enjoyed several years of prosperity before the railroad began to offer serious competition. The steamers became elegant carriages of luxury, providing the best in accommodation and comfort. One, the *Robert E. Lee,* was the undisputed Queen of the river.

Although racing was commonplace on the river no-one had ever challenged the *Lee,* possibly because she had broken several speed records without even trying, but in 1860 her supremacy was threatened by a new rival, the *Natchez.*

In that year the *Natchez* raced against the *Eclipse,* one of the largest steamers on the river and herself a record holder, and when, in 1870, the *Natchez* lowered the 26-year-old New Orlean to St. Louis record by one hour, the gauntlet was down for a race with the *Robert E. Lee.*

The vessels were fairly evenly matched. The *Lee* was 300ft long, the *Natchez* a few feet longer, and the advantage of the latter's larger paddle-wheels was offset by the *Lee*'s bigger cylinders. The day set for the race was June 20th, 1870, and when the two vessels arrived at the start, over a million dollars had been staked on the outcome of the race.

The owner-captain of the *Natchez,* Thomas Leathers, announced, with supreme confidence, that he would carry the normal load of passengers and cargo, and would make all the scheduled stops.

His opponent, John Cannon, was more prudent and carried only 75 passengers. He also arranged for coal barges to wait for him along the route so that he could refuel without stopping.

At seven minutes to five in the afternoon the *Robert E. Lee* backed away from the jetty, floated downstream a few yards and then, as her paddles bit into the water, began to move forward. The *Natchez* was still loading, and a few minutes later Captain Leathers cast off and moved out in pursuit of his rival. At St. Mary's Market, the *Lee* had a three minutes lead, but after only 30 miles she was in trouble. The pump which fed the boilers had broken down, and although it was quickly repaired it required constant attention for the rest of the voyage. This setback allowed the *Natchez* to take the lead, only to be overtaken again at nightfall.

At 1.30 a.m. the *Lee* was two miles ahead of the *Natchez*, and as they passed Baton Rouge the surrounding countryside changed from flat, open plains to dense forest.

The river became shallower and the danger from rocks and snags increased. Both vessels were now in the hands of their pilots, Enoch King on the *Lee* and Jesse Jamieson on the *Natchez*. Their domain was the tiny wheelhouse where no-one, not even the captain, was allowed when the boat was under way. Every ripple on the water, every change in shade or colour was a signal to their expert eyes. When Natchez was reached the next day the town turned out to greet its favourite, but they were disappointed. The *Robert E. Lee* was still ahead by one mile. At this point the boats refuelled, the *Lee* without stopping as planned, and the *Natchez* lost eight minutes by fuelling at the wharf. The next coaling point was Memphis and Captain Leathers, now beginning to regret his show of confidence, telegraphed to have coal-barges waiting for him also.

At Vicksburgh the *Lee* was four miles ahead. Then the *Natchez* suffered the same trouble as the *Lee* had experienced at the start of the race and when Memphis was reached she was an hour behind.

And so to the final stretch. 200 miles to St. Louis over the most treacherous part of the river. A chain of rocks, where the wrecks of over 200 steamboats lay, stood in the path of the racing steamers, and to add to the danger a thick fog descended.

Both ships stopped, but the *Lee* had taken on two pilots who were experts on this part of the river, and after an hour she moved on.

Misfortune struck again when a steampipe began to

leak and pressure had to be reduced by half. As the *Lee* groped her way out of the fog and approached St. Louis there was no way of knowing if the *Natchez* had gone ahead. The welcome at St. Louis told its own story. The *Robert E. Lee* was the victor, she had taken three days, 18 hours and 14 minutes, and this time has never been beaten. So ended one of the great adventures of the American Middle West, and it was the last big steamboat race on the Mississippi.

The legend of the Mississippi steamboats tends to overshadow the history of paddle steamers in other parts of America. But as in the old world they plied on every navigable stretch of water in the country. It was on the Delaware that John Fitch tried out his strange canoe-paddle craft twenty years before the *Clermont* was built. And when John Stevens took the *Phoenix* to Philadelphia in 1809 the Delaware became an important steamboat highway. Many companies were set up, and one, the Camden and Amboy Railroad, introduced a very novel paddle steamer, named the *John Neilson,* which incorporated a machine for providing a cushion of air beneath the hull, and this was over 100 years before the first hovercraft skimmed over the waters of Southern England.

As in Europe the American paddle steamers only survived as an important mode of travel until the railways became established. And when the automobile became popular, killing the excursion trade, the decline accelerated rapidly.

Thanks to Hollywood the younger generation probably have a better idea of what a Mississippi steamboat looked like than they have of a Thames or Clyde steamer, but even less is known of the paddle steamers which served a similar role on the Australian continent. Their story is not often told, but the paddlers 'down under' played an important part in the discovery of the 'outback' and it is a story worth telling.

The Murray River, with its many tributaries, is very similar to the Mississippi, it was once known as 'the Mississippi of New Holland', and it is the fourth largest river system in the world. It is navigable for a distance of over 3,500 miles and consists mainly of the Murray, Edwards, Wakool, Murrumbidgee and Darling rivers.

The mouth of the Murray is about sixty miles east of Adelaide, South Australia, and from there it stretches eastwards into New South Wales where its tributaries branch out on either side, the Darling driving northwards almost into Queensland.

Explorations by whaleboats in the 1830's and 40's showed that the use of the river as a means of transport and communication was a viable proposition, and in 1850 the South Australian Government offered a bonus of £4,000 to each of the first two steamboats to sail from Goolwa, at the mouth, to the Darling Junction. The offer specified that the steamboats must be iron-hulled, with a draught of not more than two feet, and with engines of more than forty horsepower.

Three years elapsed before anyone attempted to win the prize, and the two men who did so pioneered Australia's inland marine service, a trade which produced boats and men as colourful and as exciting as could be found anywhere in the world.

William Randell had never seen a steamboat when he set about building his own, nor had he heard of the Government bonus, and consequently his *Mary Ann* did not comply with the stipulations. She was wood built, 50ft long with a 9ft beam, and drew three feet of water. The engine was a mere 8 h.p. fed by a 7ft long rectangular boiler, which now stands on the bank of the Murray at Mannum. It is said that the boiler had to be lashed with chains to prevent it from bursting, and even then it breathed like an old concertina. Randell's interest in steaming up the Murray had been aroused by the

169

discovery of gold in New South Wales. A trading steamer taking supplies to the diggers and returning with wool from the sheep farms seemed to him to be a profitable enterprise, especially as the journey by bullock-wagon took over six weeks. Assisted by his brothers, Thomas and Elliott, Randell assembled his boat at Noa-No, a few miles upstream from Mannum, and in March 1853 the *Mary Ann* steamed down to Goolwa, to become the first paddle steamer on the Murray river.

The first attempted journey from Goolwa to the Darling Junction was commenced on March 25th, 1853, but after travelling 125 miles the Randells found their way blocked by an impassable sand-bar. They returned to Noa-No and waited for the river to rise.

Captain Francis Cadell was also interested in the trading possibilities of the Murray, and to him the Government bonus acted as a spur. His paddle steamer, the *Lady Augusta,* was built at Sydney, and on August 25th, 1853 she left Goolwa, with a barge in tow, for the journey up river.

Randell started out on his second attempt ten days earlier. He seems to have been unaware of Cadell's challenge, for he proceeded slowly and did not reach Darling Junction until September 3rd.

Had the *Mary Ann* qualified for the £4,000 Randell could have claimed it, but in any case, his prime objective was to open a trading route and so he pushed on. Eleven days later he passed the Murrumbidgee Junction, 770 miles from the sea, where he tied up for the night.

He was awakened during the night by a sound that only once before had been heard on that part of the river, the unmistakable sound of paddle wheels and the steady throb of a steam engine. When Randell and his crew rushed on to the deck they saw the *Lady Augusta* steaming up river at a rate of four knots. Immediately the *Mary Ann*'s furnace was lit and as soon as there was enough steam available Randell set off in pursuit of his rival.

From then on the two steamers passed and repassed each other several times, but the *Mary Ann* was the smaller of the two and when they reached Gannawarra, the *Lady Augusta* was unable to proceed any further. Randell pressed on; to Moama, 1,176 miles from the sea and only 300 miles short of Albury, the furthest town on the river.

Cadell was awarded £4,000 even though Randell had beaten him to the Darling Junction. There followed a public outcry and eventually Randell received £300 plus £450 raised by public subscriptions. Both men set up companies to trade on the river and over the ensuing years the Murray's tributaries were explored one by one. New vessels were built, some in Australian yards and others in Britain and America. Because of this the Murray riverboats did not develop into a single type as did the Mississippi steamers.

Some were side-wheelers, some were stern-wheelers, some had open decks, others had high deckhouses, much depended on what areas they were built to serve, and the type of hazards they were expected to meet.

Sand-bars were a common barrier, and there are many stories of how the intrepid skippers overcame these. The cautious ones would attach a rope to a tree on the river bank and use a winch on board to drag the boat across. If the winch was not powerful enough the rope was attached to the paddle-shaft. Others would steam full ahead at the sand-bar and try to 'leap' over it, using the paddles to scrabble across. They were a special breed, these riverboat skippers. Colourful characters with picturesque names; The Black Angel, Pirate Wilson, Midnight Johnny. They helped to open up the wide plains that are drained by the Murray Basin by feeding and clothing the settlers and transporting their produce.

Randell modified the *Mary Ann* by lengthening the

171

hull, but the vessel was still not to his satisfaction so he built another hull, joined the two together and called the resulting craft *Gemini*.

Several years later Randell separated the hulls, one was used as a barge, the other, the old *Mary Ann*'s, sank in deep water off Mannum and is still there.

The *Lady Augusta* survived until 1871, though she too was greatly modified over the years. Her hull was left on a sandbank at Echuca and gradually became covered by silt.

Despite the many hazards, serious accidents were rare. Between 1852 and the present day 218 steamers were built for the Murray and most of them lived to be a ripe old age. But they too were beaten by the enemy of paddle steamers the world over, the railways.

One riverboat which did survive was the *Murrumbidgee*. Built in 1865 she was destroyed by fire in 1948. The old-timer had undergone many changes and refits in her time, and in 1947 she was converted for passenger carrying by the Murray Valley Coaches Limited. She was so popular on excursions and fishing trips that, after her destruction, her owners decided to replace her with a new vessel. Using an old barge, the 'J. L. Roberts', the paddle wheels from the *Excelsior,* and the shafting from the *Murrumbidgee,* they built a diesel-powered paddle boat which they called the *Coonawarra*. The *Coonawarra,* the Aboriginal name for Black Swan, still plys the lower waters of the Murray and trips are booked well in advance. Her hybrid construction makes her a positive link with the past, and as she glides between the Red Gum trees, on one of the world's most beautiful waterways, the spirits of the *Mary Ann*, the *Lady Augusta* and a genera-ation of riverboatmen go with her.

L.N.E.R. STEAMER, JEANIE DEANS.

Fig. 20 — The JEANIE DEANS. Renamed QUEEN OF THE SOUTH she was
the last paddle steamer to operate commercially on the Thames.
(Photo Glasgow Museums and Art Galleries).

Fig. 21 — The OLD CALEDONIA, now a floating 'pub' and restaurant, sits at her new berth on the Thames. (Photo courtesy of Bass Charrington Ltd.).

Chapter Sixteen

UNDER THE WHITE ENSIGN

Royal Navy paddle vessels — Frigates and Sloops — H.M.S. *Terrible* — The *Birkenhead* disaster — *Alecto* v *Rattler* — Paddle warships decline — The role of paddle steamers in two World Wars — The Dunkirk evacuation.

THE Royal Navy, with its long and proud tradition of 'wooden-wall' sailing ships, was slow to accept the idea of steam propulsion, and when it did so the first steps were taken cautiously. Henry Bell, designer of the *Comet*, tried to interest the Admiralty in steamships in 1800, but his suggestion was rebuffed, although it is said that Nelson recognised the possibilities. When, at last, their Lordships did agree to purchase a steamship it was a dispatch boat, the idea of a steam warship still being very far from their minds. The engineers John Rennie and Marc Brunel were instrumental in persuading the Admiralty to order the building of a new vessel. Named H.M.S. *Comet* and launched at Deptford in 1822, the ship was a wooden paddle steamer of 238 tons powered by engines of 80 n.h.p. Later she was joined by the *Monkey*, a similar vessel built at Rotherhithe in 1821, but not to the orders of the Admiralty.

These pioneers were followed by other vessels which were used as tugs or dispatch boats and were only lightly armed, if they were armed at all. By the end of the 1820's several paddle steamers were flying the White Ensign, but they were a motley collection as the Admiralty had no official designs for tugs or dispatch boats, this being left entirely to the contractors.

The situation began to improve in 1830 when Sir James Graham replaced Lord Melville as First Lord of the Admiralty. In 1831 a dispatch vessel, named H.M.S. *Black Eagle,* was launched and she was armed with a single 18-pounder gun. Her side-lever engines were of 140 n.h.p., but later these were replaced by direct-acting oscillating engines of 260 h.p. which gave the vessel a speed of 11 knots. The Surveyor to the Navy began to design steamers for the Service in 1832 and although these were still only intended for miscellaneous duties their armament was increased to three or four guns.

Steam warships, in the true sense of the word, began to appear in 1837 with the launching of the paddle frigate H.M.S. *Gorgon.* She was designed by Sir W. Symonds and was fitted with direct-acting engines which are fully described in Chapter Nine. The *Gorgon* was teak built with oak main beams and weighed 1,111 tons. Her length was 178ft, breadth 37ft 6 inches and the paddle-wheels were 27ft in diameter. She carried two 10 inch and four thirty-pounder guns on the upper deck and had a complement of 160 men. In 1840 H.M.S. *Gorgon* went into action with three paddle sloops, *Vesuvius, Stromboli* and *Phoenix,* in the bombardment of Acre under the command of Admiral Stopford.

Paddle sloops appeared in 1838 when H.M.S. *Acheron,* also designed by Symonds, was launched at Sheerness. Her side-lever engines gave a speed of 10 knots and her armament comprised two 9-pounder guns. Frigates and sloops continued to be built of wood, although iron was already being used for the construction of commercial vessels.

In 1836 John Laird designed an iron-built frigate and the ship was launched at Birkenhead in 1842. The Admiralty, however, were not convinced that iron was a suitable material for ships of the line and the vessel was sold to Mexico. The Admiralty's rejection of iron may seem odd as one of the problems connected with paddle warships was the vulnerability of the paddle-wheels. Nevertheless wooden frigates were built to increasingly large dimensions, and a typical vessel of the 1840's was of 1,400 tons with a length of 210ft and a breadth of 40ft. Armament consisted of 32 guns carried on two decks, and in addition, two guns on traversing carriages were placed fore and aft on the upper deck. The engines were usually side-lever giving a speed of between 7 and 10 knots. The largest paddle frigate of that period was H.M.S. *Terrible,* one of the most powerful steam warships of her time. Designed by Oliver Lang, the *Terrible* was 226ft long with a beam of 42.5ft.

The hull was built to carry heavy armament and machinery and so closely fitted was the framework that the vessel was watertight before the fitting of the external planking. Her engines were of 2,059 indicated horsepower and were of the twin cylinder type similar to the 'Siamese' engine described in Chapter Nine.

The original armament of H.M.S. *Terrible* comprised twenty guns; four 56-pounders, four 68-pounders on each of her two decks, plus three 12-pounders and a field gun. She played an active part in the Crimean War when her firepower was used to good effect at the seige of Sevastopol.

Despite the Admiralty's doubts as to the suitability of iron for warships they ordered an iron-built frigate in 1845. She was named *Birkenhead* and was launched at that town in 1846. Shortly after she went into service the Admiralty carried out experiments on an iron vessel to determine the effect of gunfire on iron plating.

As a result of these tests the *Birkenhead* was reclassified as a troopship, and it was while she was serving in this capacity that she was wrecked in one of the greatest disasters in naval history.

On January 7th, 1852, the *Birkenhead* left Cork bound for South Africa. On board were officers and men from ten regiments, twenty-five women and thirty-one children, which with the crew totalled 680. At Simonstown some of the women and children were landed, leaving twenty on board, and the ship then proceeded for Port Elizabeth where the troops were to be put ashore.

It was a clear night and, although the ship was a good distance from the land, the lights ashore could easily be seen. Look-outs were on duty and the leadsman was taking regular soundings as the ship proceeded at a steady speed of 8 knots.

Suddenly the call "By the deep twelve" indicated that the water had shallowed to a depth of twelve fathoms. The leadsman hastily started to take another sounding, but before he could take the reading the *Birkenhead* crashed on to a reef of rocks. Soundings taken from the stern showed that there was sixty feet of water there and the Master, Captain Salmond, ordered the engines to be put astern. The result was disastrous, for a pinnacle of rock had pierced the hull and the action of going astern ripped a hole in the ship's bottom. Within minutes the lower decks were flooded, including the magazine which prevented any hope of signalling for help by firing the guns. The boats were lowered and all the women and children were saved, but for the rest there was little hope. The funnel crashed to the deck, killing two men, and the stern lifted out of the water before plunging to the bottom as the ship broke in two. Twenty-five minutes after the crash the *Birkenhead* had gone, leaving the sea sprinkled with a mass of struggling bodies.

Some managed to swim ashore, but most were drowned or met a terrible end, for the water was infested with man-eating sharks.

The Admiralty strongly believed in practical demonstrations to prove, or disprove, theories concerning the

176

development of naval vessels. One such demonstration, in which the paddle steamers H.M.S. *Helicon* and H.M.S. *Salamis* took part, showed the superiority of the project-ing cutwater, or 'plough bow'. The *Helicon* was modified to incorporate this idea and in 1865 a number of trials showed that she was faster than her sister ship by 1 to 1½ knots. Another experiment, carried out twenty years earlier, was an important turning point in the history of naval architecture, for it marked the beginning of the end for paddle warships.

Screw propulsion was first brought to the attention of the Admiralty by a Swedish engineer, John Ericsson, in 1836. But Ericsson's idea did not appeal to them, in spite of a practical demonstration on the Thames, as they considered that a vessel propelled at the stern would be unsteerable.

In 1843, however, the Admiralty had second thoughts and ordered that a paddle sloop, still under construction, should be converted to screw propulsion. The vessel was named H.M.S. *Rattler,* and after experimenting with various screw designs it was decided to carry out tests against a paddle vessel of similar size and power. H.M.S. *Alecto* was chosen as the adversary for the new ship and a series of races took place. The *Rattler* won the first one easily, over a distance of eighty miles and in calm condi-tions she was home twenty-three and a half minutes before her rival. A second race, over a shorter course, resulted in another win for the *Rattler,* and when in a third race with sea and wind against them, the *Alecto* was beaten by a clear forty minutes the superiority of the screw had been clearly demonstrated. One more test was held, for the supporters of paddle propulsion main-tained that the paddle steamer had the advantage of better towing power, and so a tug-of-war was arranged between the two vessels.

The *Alecto* held her own for a few minutes, but slowly

the *Rattler* began to gain the ascendancy and her struggling rival was dragged ignominiously astern at a speed of 2½ knots. This test, although apparently conclusive, was a little unfair, for despite the fact the both ship's engines had the same nominal horsepower, the *Rattler*'s engines had an indicated horsepower of 300 against the *Alecto*'s 141.

Nevertheless the screw had made its impact, and although the paddle-wheel remained in favour on tugs and dispatch boats the Navy's warships soon adopted screw propulsion. Apart from its efficiency the propellor had other advantages, it was protected from gunfire, its driving engines could be placed below the water-line and the absence of paddle-boxes allowed a more favourable positioning of the guns.

Paddle steamers, however, made a comeback in World War 1, when they were used in a variety of roles. The Admiralty took over many of the pleasure steamers and used them as troop-carriers, supply ships, minelayers, and minesweepers, and it was in the latter role that they really excelled themselves. So much so that the Admiralty built a fleet of paddle-minesweepers which became known as the *Ascot* class. The first was H.M.S. *Ascot,* 245.75ft long and propelled by 1,400 h.p. inclined compound engines. She had two twelve-pounder guns and carried two seaplanes. Thirty-two vessels of this class were built, all bearing the names of racecourses.

The majority of the larger shipping companies contributed paddle steamers, and their crews, to war service, and many were involved in heroic escapades.

The Isle of Man Steam Packet Company's *Mona's Queen* sank a U-boat in the English Channel in February, 1917. She was on a voyage from Southampton to Havre when she spotted a submarine on the surface. A torpedo was fired at the steamer before the U-boat hastily began to submerge, but the missile passed harmlessly by and before the submarine could dive to safety her upperworks were caught in the *Mona's Queen's* port paddle-wheel, causing so much damage that she flooded and sank immediately. The G.S.N. Company's *Golden Eagle* served as a troopship and seaplane carrier and carried a total of 518,101 troops and other units between 1915 and and 1919. The Company's *Eagle* was renamed *Aiglon* and served as a minesweeper from 1915 until 1920.

Some paddle steamers found themselves in foreign waters many hundreds of miles from their natural habitat.

The 'Belle' steamers *Walton Belle* and *London Belle,* after a period of minesweeping off the French and Danish coasts, were fitted out as hospital ships and were sent to the White Sea, a distance of over 2,000 miles from the Thames. The trip took twenty days and the two vessels served in the Arctic Seas around Archangel for four months before returning home.

The war years took a heavy toll of paddle steamers, for although their shallow draught made them ideally suited for minesweeping they stood little chance of survival if a mine was struck. Many of those that came through un-scathed were unfit for further use unless large sums of money were spent on their refurbishing, and with the trade already in a decline few owners were prepared to make such an investment. Consequently when war came again in 1939 there were fewer paddle steamers available to discard their company colours for Admiralty Grey.

Nevertheless many did so, some for the second time. The last task carried out by the G.S.N. steamers before dispersing into their various roles was to help in the evacuation of London's children. During the first three days of September 1939, eight steamers carried 19,578 children from Gravesend, Dagenham and Tilbury to the relative safety of Felixstowe, Lowestoft and Great Yarmouth.

As in the First World War the main task allotted to the

paddle steamers was minesweeping. But another useful function carried out by some of the larger ships was that of anti-aircraft vessels. The *Royal Eagle* had a very impressive record in this type of activity, and a Daily Telegraph report of 1st August, 1943, showed that she had been in action 52 times, had shot down two aircraft and saved 24 lives. The Clyde diesel-electric paddler *Talisman* also worked as an anti-aircraft ship on the Thames under the name of H.M.S. *Aristocrat*.

Later in the war she took part in the raid on Dieppe and was H.Q. ship at the construction of the Mulberry Harbour on the north coast of France. Other Clyde steamers that left their native Scotland were the *Caledonia, Waverley, Jeanie Deans, Marmion,* and *Mercury*. The *Marmion* was a 'second-timer', but was bombed and sunk at Harwich in April 1941. The *Mercury* struck a mine while on patrol with the *Caledonia* off the south coast of Ireland. She was taken in tow by her partner but sank a few miles out from Milford Haven. Even the ancient *Madge Wildfire* played her part. The fifty-year-old ship, now called *Fair Maid,* was beyond active service but was transformed into a decontamination vessel.

It was in 1940, however, that the paddle steamers had their finest hour. The story of the Dunkirk evacuation has been told many times. How the beleaguered men of the British Expeditionary Force were snatched to safety from the beaches with the advancing German army only a few miles away.

Every vessel capable of going to sea rallied to form a great armada of 'little ships', and the part played by the paddle steamers was of major importance. Many memories of a trip to Southend or a cruise down the Clyde must have been evoked as the battle-weary troops saw those familiar names, *Medway Queen, Crested Eagle, Duchess of Fife, Waverley*. Time and time again they returned to defy the German dive-bombers. The *Royal Eagle* made three trips, was dive-bombed 43 times and rescued 3,000 men. The *Golden Eagle* brought back over 2,000 troops and on her first trip she picked up the survivors of the *Waverley* which had been bombed and sunk. On her second trip she was off Dunkirk for an hour while her two boats ferried men from the shore. During this time she was under constant air attack but her anti-aircraft guns kept the enemy at bay. Later she came under heavy artillery fire and she moved inside the harbour, only to come under attack again by about fifty enemy aircraft.

Her last trip was made at night, but by this time the position had become very difficult. She managed to get alongside the pier, but picked up no one and as the block ships were moving into position she left for home, the last ship, apart from a destroyer, to do so.

The *Crested Eagle* was less fortunate. She was one of the first to arrive at Dunkirk in the company of a trawler, a destroyer and an Irish cross-channel vessel. There were no troops ready to go on board and the German planes were attacking at intervals of about twenty minutes.

The trawler was destroyed first, followed by the Irish vessel and finally the destroyer. The *Crested Eagle* took on as many men as she could and began to move away from the area. Again the Germans returned to the attack and the paddle steamer was struck at the after end of her engine room.

Her captain kept her running along the coast, but very soon she became a blazing inferno and had to be beached. Two ships belonging to the New Medway Steam Packet Company were busily engaged during this time. The *Queen of Thanet,* after making two trips, went to the aid of a disabled steamer which had 3,000 men on board. 2,000 were taken on board the paddle steamer, which then returned to Margate before proceeding once more to the Dunkirk beaches.

In all the *Queen of Thanet* rescued 4,000 men. Her sister ship, the *Medway Queen,* made seven trips and brought back 7,000 men; more than any other ship below the size of a destroyer. On one trip she rescued all the troops and crew from the *Brighton Belle* which had struck a submerged wreck. These were some of the outstanding feats achieved by the paddlers that went to Dunkirk. Many others played their part.

The *Princess Elizabeth* rescued 1,763 men, including 500 French soldiers. The Clyde steamer *Eagle III* was beached and used as a temporary landing stage. Even the Woolwich Ferry steamer, *John Benn,* tried to get to Dunkirk, but had to turn back because of mechanical troubles.

At the end of the operation many fine paddle steamers had gone. The *Gracie Fields, Brighton Queen, Waverley* and *Devonia* were among the casualties. Yet the miracle of Dunkirk had been achieved, and that so many paddle steamers survived is a miracle in itself.

After their moment of glory the paddlers returned to their normal wartime duties, which although less dramatic were no less hazardous. Without the armour plating and heavy armament of warships they were always vulnerable. As in the First World War many fell victims to mines, and German bombers were a new menace that had to be faced.

When caught on patrol they were sitting ducks for an air attack, and paddle steamers which were lost in this way included the veteran Clyde steamer *Kylemore,* the *Juno* and the South Coast steamer *Her Majesty.*

During the London Blitz the humble Woolwich Ferries took part in an operation in which they served nobly. On the night of September 7th, 1940, the north bank of the Thames was ablaze and many areas were cut off. The ferry boats carried hundreds of Londoners to safety, dodging patches of blazing oil and floating debris, a gallant action which saved many lives.

When the war ended the ranks of the paddle steamers were thinned even further, the inevitable scrappings taking their toll. The owners, remembering the pre-war decline, looked to the future with cautious optimism. But whatever the future held for the paddle steamers they had secured for themselves a glorious place in British Naval history.

Chapter Seventeen

THE TWILIGHT YEARS

The post-war years — new paddlers — the decline accelerates —
first efforts at preservation — *Compton Castle* — *Medway
Queen* — *Princess Elizabeth* — A tug goes to San Francisco —
The Continental scene — *Caledonia* preserved — New hopes for
the future.

IN the immediate post-war years Britain's major coastal
resorts made great efforts to get back to peace-time conditions, despite rationing and the many restrictions that
still applied. The paddle steamer operators took stock of
their fleets and began to make preparations for the
summer excursion trade. There were numerous problems
to be faced. Many of the steamers were worn out, piers
had been cut to prevent their use in the event of an in-
vasion, and some areas had not been completely cleared
of mines.

A succession of wet and chilly summers dampened the
prospects of a boom and petrol rationing did not prevent
serious competition from motor-coaches and the private
cars.

Where paddle steamers were an essential communications link the services had been maintained throughout
the war, and with the post-war rush to 'get away from it
all', the steamers on the Isle of Wight, Isle of Man and
some Clyde routes were under heavy pressure.

Excursion trips were limited to relatively short runs,
and on the South Coast and in the West Country they
enjoyed a short period of popularity. The Thames

steamers also did well for a time with their trips to the Kent and Essex resorts, although the G.S.N.'s motor vessels *Royal Sovereign* and the *Royal Daffodil* had become the favourites with trippers. They were faster than their paddle sisters, and perhaps Londoners had no wish to gaze upon the devastated banks of their river for any longer than was necessary.

After the scrapping of the war-worn vessels the total number of passenger-carrying paddle steamers in Britain in 1946 was 55, and this number included the first of the very few paddle steamers to be built after the war.

The *Bristol Queen* was launched on April 4th, 1946, to join the Bristol Channel Fleet of P & A Campbell. Campbells had suffered badly as a result of the war, losing seven of their ships, and they planned to purchase four new vessels to replace those lost. In fact, only two were built, the *Cardiff Queen* joining the fleet in 1947. Both 'Queens' were similar in design, the *Bristol Queen* being the larger of the two. She was built by Charles Hill and Son at Bristol and was 244.7ft long with a beam of 59.8ft over the concealed paddle-boxes.

The *Cardiff Queen* was built by Fairfields and was 240ft long by 59.7ft in beam. Both vessels had triple-expansion engines, giving a speed of 16 knots, and were oil-fired.

1947 also saw the first post-war withdrawal. The 45-year-old *Solent,* one of the Lymington-Isle of Wight ferries. This tiny veteran, 135.5ft long and 20.2ft in beam, had been used to tow car-carrying barges before the introduction of double-ended motor vessels. She did not go to the breakers yards immediately as she was purchased for use as a floating cafe and dance hall. When planning permission for this project was refused she was beached at Porchester close to the road which runs between Portsmouth and Fareham. Here she served as a lorry-drivers' dormitory before being broken up in 1959.

In Scotland another new paddle steamer went into service in 1947. This was the *Waverley*, built for the London and North Eastern Railway to replace the vessel of the same name that was lost at Dunkirk. The *Waverley* has all the characteristics of a modern paddler, cruiser stern, raked bow and not concealed paddle-boxes. She is, nevertheless, a handsome vessel of 693 gross tons, 235.3ft in length with a beam of 30.2ft. Her triple expansion engines give her a speed of 17 knots.

In 1948 two more paddle steamers were withdrawn. The Southampton Company's *Solent Queen* and the South Western Steam Navigation Company's *Pride of Devon*. The latter we have met before in this book, for she was originally the *Walton Belle*, built in 1897. She later became the *Essex Queen* with the New Medway Steam Packet Company, and took her final name in 1945. She was the longest lived of all the original 'Belle' steamers.

No less than six paddle steamers were withdrawn in 1949, four of them being among the best-known in the country. The Clyde steamer *Lucy Ashton*, Cosens' famous *Monarch* and the G.S.N. Co.'s *Golden Eagle* and *Royal Eagle*. The other two steamers were the *Duchess of Cornwall*, owned by the Southampton Co., and the River Forth car ferry *Dundee*.

The departure of the 'Eagles' ended the era of the big paddlers on the Thames. *Royal Eagle* was the largest paddle steamer in Britain during the post-war years, but she could not compete with the motor vessels for speed, although many would claim that her passenger facilities were equal to anything offered by the newer vessels.

The *Monarch* had the unique distinction, for a paddle steamer, of serving the same owner for the whole of her 62 years lifetime. The *Lucy Ashton* was built in 1888, the same year as the *Monarch*, and served on the Clyde continuously.

During the Second World War she operated alone from Craigendoran, keeping the vital services open for 6½ years. After withdrawal her hull was used by the British Shipbuilding Research Association for experiments with jet engines.

Between 1950 and 1960 twenty more paddle steamers were withdrawn, all eventually to be scrapped, but one more true paddle steamer was built in 1953. When the Loch Lomond steamer *Princess May* was withdrawn, in 1952, it was intended to replace her with two diesel-screw vessels. The shallow draught required in certain parts of the Loch, however, could be achieved only in a paddle steamer, and so an order was placed with A & J Inglis for a ship that was to be the largest ever to sail on British inland waters.

The vessel was prefabricated at Pointhouse, Glasgow, and assembled at Balloch on Loch Lomond, where she was launched on 5th March, 1953, and given the name *Maid of the Loch*. She was the last big paddle steamer to be built in Europe, possibly in the world, and is one of the few still running. Her dimensions are 191.0ft by 28.1ft, with compound diagonal engines giving a speed of 12 knots. She is modern in appearance, with a single funnel and twin masts, but as a refreshing change her paddle-boxes are clearly defined. A spacious full-length promenade deck, observation lounges, dining saloons and a cafeteria provide accommodation for 1,000 passengers. For a while she ran in conjunction with the only other steamer on the Loch, the *Prince Edward,* but that vessel was broken up in 1955 and from then on the *Maid of the Loch* has operated alone.

The distinction of being the very last steam paddler to be built in Britain goes to the tiny *Cleddau Queen.* An ungainly craft, built for a special purpose, she was owned by the Pembrokeshire County Council and used by them on the Pembroke Dock to Neyland Ferry, across the

Cleddau estuary. Only six years after her launching in 1956 she was joined on the service by a twin-screw diesel ferry, and it soon became apparent that the *Cleddau Queen* was vastly inferior to the more modern vessel. The cost of replacing her was too great and she continued in service until 1968, when she was converted to diesel-screw propulsion.

By the end of 1960 the total numbers of paddle steamers in Britain had been reduced by half, and lovers of these fine ships watched their going in helpless dismay.

It seemed inevitable that before long the sight and sound of a paddler threshing its way down river, or swanning gracefully up to a pier, would soon be gone forever. Yet what could be done? It had to be admitted that they were inefficient compared with diesel powered vessels, and in any case, the excursion trade was in a decline, regardless of what type of vessel was used. One cannot help feeling that some of the larger steamship companies could have kept and preserved at least one of the ships that had served them so well, but there is no room for sentiment in business apparently, and it was left to private individuals and concerns to come to the rescue of the paddle steamer.

In 1961-62 four more paddlers were withdrawn, among them the *Compton Castle* which became the first to be taken over and restored two years later, and in 1963 six were destined to go to the breakers, including all of the Woolwich ferries, and the veteran Thames steamer, *Medway Queen*. When the withdrawal of the latter was announced it was realised by many that here was a ship that had to be saved. Apart from her fine war record she was typical of so many of the river and coastal paddlers. Several bodies, the Dunkirk Veterans Association among them, banded together to form the 'Medway Queen Trust'. It was not possible to keep her in an operational state and in 1964, she was purchased by Fortes, the catering concern, for use as a floating restaurant on the Thames. Planning permission was refused and the ship was sold to a Belgian firm of breakers for a sum of £7,500.

A last minute reprieve came when three Isle of Wight businessmen, headed by Mr. Alan Ridett, raised £6,000. Messrs. Van Heyghen, the breakers, generously relinquished their option, and on 7th September, 1965, the *Medway Queen* was towed to the Isle of Wight. She is now the centrepiece of an impressive yacht haven on the River Medina known as the Medway Queen Yacht Marina. Her engines, though stilled and silent, are intact. The saloons have been converted into dining rooms, bars and a small dance hall. The ship is open to the public during the summer months and temporary membership of the club is obtainable for a moderate fee.

And so another paddle steamer was saved, and at last their total extinction had been averted.

At the end of the summer season of 1965 the Isle of Wight ferry steamer *Sandown* was withdrawn, and ended her days in a breakers' yard at Antwerp. In the West Country the *Princess Elizabeth* was about to start on the last stages of her chequered career. After her brief period at Torquay the *Princess Elizabeth* went to Weymouth in 1963 to replace the *Consul*. She stayed there until 1966 when she was sold to a Sussex businessman for use as a floating casino. The project failed before it started and the ship was sold to a firm of breakers at Weymouth who removed the engines. It seemed as though the *Princess Elizabeth* was doomed, but yet another use was planned for her. The tremendous popularity of boating and yachting caused a number of yacht marina projects to be proposed on the South Coast.

Following the example of the Isle of Wight concern, a company was formed to set up a yacht marina on Hayling Island, with the *Princess Elizabeth* as the centrepiece. The vessel was towed to the Hampshire resort and was beached there pending planning permission being granted. Permission was refused, and once again the ship seemed to be destined for the breakers' yards. For two years she lay on the beach at Hayling Island before she attracted the attention of a London pleasure boat operator, Mr. Don Hickman. Mr. Hickman purchased her, and on 4th June, 1970, exactly 30 years to the hour after her Dunkirk rescue operation, she was towed to the Thames by the German tug *Fairplay*. A berth was provided at the St. Katharine Dock, only a few yards from Tower Pier which was once used by the G.S.N. paddle steamers.

Here she has been fitted out as a floating restaurant and conference centre and will form part of the mammoth St. Katharine-by-the-Tower redevelopment scheme. The absence of her boilers has provided space for the luxuriously appointed Conference Hall. Her saloons have been converted to bars and a restaurant, and in the engine room a small museum has been set up to commemorate the epic of Dunkirk. The ship is open to the public all the year round and the Conference Hall has already been used by several appropriately interested bodies, such as the Dunkirk Veterans Association.

Among the four paddle steamers withdrawn in 1966 was the *Cardiff Queen,* only twenty years old and the first post-war built paddler to go out of service. Her sister, the *Bristol Queen,* followed in 1967.

Also in 1966 the diesel-electric *Talisman* finally ended her days. The combination of diesel-electric motors and paddle-wheels had not been a great success, and it is remarkable that her owners put up with her temperamental failings for so long. Even so she was re-engined in 1954 and it may be that her passenger capacity of 1,253 weighed in her favour.

A brave attempt to revive the Thames paddle steamer service was made in 1966 when the newly formed Coastal

Steam Packet Company bought the famous Clyde steamer *Jeanie Deans*.

She was scheduled to sail daily from Tower Pier to Clacton and Herne Bay under a new name, *Queen of the South*. The *Jeanie Deans* was no stranger to the Thames.

She had served as an Anti-Aircraft vessel there in 1941, and it was during this time that she raced against, and beat, the *Royal Eagle*, thus demolishing the latter's claim to be the fastest paddle steamer in the world. The *Queen of the South,* however, was only a shadow of her former self. Throughout the season she was constantly plagued with boiler and paddle-wheel troubles. The Coastal Steam Packet Company ran into debt and was wound up in September 1967, and the *Queen of the South/Jeanie Deans* went to the breakers' yard in December.

On the South Coast only one paddle steamer now remained in service, the Isle of Wight ferry, *Ryde*. Since the end of the war she had been confined to the Solent crossing, but in 1968 she was chartered to operate on the Thames as a floating 'Gin Palace'.

The manufacturers of Gilbey's Gin used her for a series of publicity cruises, after which she returned to Portsmouth to be laid up. For a while she sat disconsolately at her moorings in Portsmouth Harbour, an object of curiosity or nostalgia for holidaymakers, depending on their ages. Then, in October 1969, she joined the *Medway Queen* in the Isle of Wight, and now sits close to her illustrious companion; another paddle steamer in honourable retirement.

The number of passenger paddle steamers operating in Britain could now be counted on one hand. In Scotland the *Caledonia* was withdrawn at the end of the 1969 season, leaving the *Waverley* as the only paddle steamer on the Clyde. But on the North East Coast three steamers still survive.

The *Lincoln Castle, Tattershall Castle* and *Wingfield*

Castle operate the Humber Ferry between Hull and New Holland, and are scheduled to remain in service until the completion of the Humber Bridge sometime in the mid-seventies. *Tattershall* and *Wingfield* are sisters, built in 1934 by William Grey and Co., at West Hartlepools. 199.9ft in length and 33.1ft beam they are powered by triple-expansion engines, giving a speed of 10 knots. Twenty cars can be carried on the aft deck and 1,200 passengers are catered for in the forward saloons and on the promenade deck.

The *Lincoln Castle* was built in 1940 by A. & J. Inglis of Glasgow and is very similar, though not identical, to her fellows. At one time these vessels were threatened by replacement by screw vessels, but the decision to build a bridge gave them a new lease of life and it is likely that they will be the last salt-water paddle steamers operating in Europe.

So far we have dealt with the fortunes of the passenger paddle steamers, the best-known to the general public, but there were other paddle vessels still doing useful work, particularly the paddle tugs.

The interesting fact about paddle tugs is that the majority of them were powered by side-lever engines. None of this type were built after 1914, therefore all those that survived the Second World War were over 30 years old, and several were over 50 years old.

In 1946 there were 59 paddle tugs operating in Britain. They were concentrated mainly on the upper Clyde, the Mersey, the Manchester Ship Canal and on the North-East Coast. During the post-war years they gradually gave way to diesel-screw tugs, but three have survived and each one is notable in its own way.

The *Eppleton Hall* was the last side-lever tug to be built in Britain. She was launched in 1914 at the South Shields yards of Hepple & Co. Ltd. Her last operational days were spent at Seaham, until she was sold for scrap in

1967 and sailed to the Tyne to await demolition. Over a year later an American newspaper proprietor, Mr. Scott Newhall, bought her for £2,500, and spent £60,000 on having her completely rebuilt. On 18th September, 1969, the *Eppleton Hall* left Newcastle to make the long voyage to San Francisco. The journey took six months and was not without incident. In the Bay of Biscay she ran out of fuel, and much of the journey was made under sail. The shortest route across the Atlantic was taken, from the Canary Islands to Gyana, and from there she proceeded to Trinidad and then through the Panama Canal to the Western Seaboard of America.

The total distance covered was 10,400 miles, a tremendous achievement for a vessel only 100ft long and a tribute to her builders. She is now cared for by the San Francisco Maritime Museum and is moored at Fisherman's Wharf along with other historic craft.

The *Reliant* was the last paddle tug to operate in Britain, and is the oldest of the surviving three. Built in 1907 by J. T. Eltringham & Co. at South Shields, she was originally named *Old Trafford* and worked on the Manchester Ship Canal. In 1956 she operated alongside the *Eppleton Hall* at Seaham, until the latter's withdrawal, when the *Reliant* was put into reserve. Unlike her companion, the *Reliant* was ear-marked for preservation as soon as she was withdrawn. At one time she was sought by the San Francisco Museum, but the National Maritime Museum stepped in to keep the vessel in Britain and in 1969 she moved south to Gravesend.

In 1971 she was cut into sections which were then reassembled inside the Neptune Hall of the Greenwich Museum where she forms the centrepiece. Her side-lever engines slowly revolve, driven by a powerful electric motor, and the port paddle-wheel can be seen in motion, clearly demonstrating the feathering action of her wooden floats. Walkways are provided through the engine room and boiler room so that visitors can see her machinery at close hand.

The third surviving paddle tug, the *John H. Amos,* was one of the few fitted with compound diagonal engines. She was launched in 1931 and was the last steam paddle tug to be built in Britain. Her owners, the Tees Conservancy Commissioners intended to use her for towing a floating crane, but she lacked the necessary power and spent most of her life doing odd jobs around the port.

In 1968 she was transferred to the Dorman Museum in Middlesbrough where she is being renovated for use as a floating maritime museum.

Other miscellaneous paddle vessels which should be mentioned are the Isle of Wight car ferry *Farringford,* a diesel powered paddler still in operation between Lymington and Yarmouth, and the *Dartmouth Higher Ferry.* The Dartmouth vessel is, in reality, a floating bridge powered by a diesel-electric motor. Two supercharged diesel engines generate the power for the electric motor, the vessel has no sponsons or paddle-boxes and the non-feathering paddle-wheels are covered only by splash guards.

One other unique vessel, which seems to have been forgotten, is the *Comet* replica of 1962. To mark the 150th Anniversary of Henry Bell's first successful journey in a paddle steamer a replica was built, using the original hull plans, on the Clyde.

On 1st September, 1962, the *Comet* sailed from Port Glasgow to Helenburgh and back carrying local dignitaries dressed in period costume. Later she appeared at the London Boat Show, and when she returned to the Clyde it was intended that she should be housed in a museum. Regrettably this did not happen, and the *Comet* has since languished in a warehouse at Port Glasgow. Perhaps the new interest in paddle steamers which has been aroused in recent years will ensure that before long she is on view again, but it is sad to think that Clydeside has apparently forgotten that it was there that the British paddle steamer was born.

In other countries the paddle steamers fared little better in the post-war years. In addition to the hybrid *Coonawarra,* Australia has the *Marion,* now used as a folklore museum on the Murray river.

America's famous stern-wheelers have all but disappeared, but legislation by President Nixon himself has ensured that at least one Mississippi steamer will continue to operate for another three years. She is the *Delta Queen,* built in 1926 and fitted with engines built by Denny Brothers of Dumbarton. On the Hudson River the *Alexander Hamilton* still survives as the last of the great side-wheelers. This vessel is probably the largest paddle steamer in the world, with an overall length of 338ft and a gross tonnage of 2,367. She is powered by an inclined triple expansion engine of 3,900 h.p. Daily cruises from New York up the Hudson to Bear Mountain are undertaken and she can carry 4,000 passengers on her triple decks.

On the European Continent things are a little better. The lakes of Switzerland and Italy are still plied by a number of paddlers, and the Rhine fleet, though drastically reduced by Allied action during the war, includes six fine paddle steamers.

The scenic beauty of these areas, combined with the fascination of travelling in these graceful vessels, attracts many visitors and a few details of the services are worth mentioning. In Switzerland there are five paddlers on Lake Geneva, five on Lake Lucerne, two on Lake Zurich and one on Lake Thun and Lake Brienz. Italy has two on Lake Como and Lake Garda, and one on Lake Maggiore. All operate regular services during the summer months and the passenger facilities are outstandingly good. Totally unlike the typical British steamers, the Continental paddlers owe more to the Hudson River steamers in their appearance, with gracefully curving sponsons, ornately decorated bows and multiple decks.

The use of the paddle-wheel was revived in Britain in 1962, appropriately on a canal. The Kennet and Avon which connects the Thames to the Bristol Channel, was closed in 1950 through serious disrepair. But a Trust was formed to re-open the 150-year-old waterway and in 1960 passenger services were started.

A retired Naval officer. Lt. Commander Wray-Bliss, built a steel vessel powered by a diesel engine driving side paddle-wheels. He called the craft *Charlotte Dundas*. 36 passengers can be accommodated on the open deck, and after six years of operating between Bath and Bathampton the vessel was transferred to Devizes, from where she runs cruises along the canal to Pewsey. In 1968 Lt. Commander Wray-Bliss built another, and larger, paddler for the Bath-Bathampton service, which he named *Jane Austen*. She has a covered saloon for 48 passengers, the paddle wheels are set into the hull at the stern and are driven by the power unit originally used in the *Charlotte Dundas*.

In 1970 the concern regarding the fate of the paddle steamers gained impetus. The *Waverley,* after a near disastrous season during which she once grounded and also had a serious altercation with Arrochar Pier, seemed certain not to sail again after her passenger licence expired in February 1972.

But her 1971 season was much more successful, great pains having been taken to improve her appearance and facilities. At the end of the season it was announced that £35,000 would be spent in order to ensure that the *Waverley* would remain in service for at least another four years. It is hoped that when she comes to the end of her time, as of course she must, some suitable use will be found for her on the Clyde, for in December 1971 the only other existing Clyde paddler, the *Old Caledonia,* left the yards of Arnott, Young to find a new berth on the Thames. The *Old Caledonia,* the 'Old' had been added by her last owners, was purchased by the brewing firm of Bass Charrington for use as a floating 'pub' and restaurant. The new owners have found that, despite her two years sojourn, she is in very good condition. Every attempt has been made to maintain and restore her character.

The distinctive 30's style decor in the saloons and lounges, red plush seats, mahogany panelling and wrought iron balustrades, has been carefully preserved. The two deck saloons have been refitted, one as a restaurant, the other as a coffee and soft drinks bar. One happy feature is that her engines and controls are intact. The engines and paddle-wheels can be seen behind glass panels, and diners can also visit the bridge where everything is as it was when the ship was in service. She is berthed at what is probably the most attractive part of London's river, just west of Waterloo Bridge on the North Bank. Her large observation windows afford a magnificent view of the Royal Festival Hall on the port side, with the Savoy Hotel and the Embankment to starboard. The ship is open to the public throughout the day.

And that, then, is the paddle steamer scene in 1973. Not as many would have wished it, but better than many would have dared hope a few years ago. The recent formation of the National Maritime Trust gives further hope that all of the five remaining operational vessels will be saved. So many of our great ships of the past have survived, *Victory, Cutty Sark, Great Britain* and the cruiser *Belfast.* The paddle steamer, as a type, played a vital part in Britain's maritime history. Already some of the finest examples have been lost forever. We must preserve what is left.

ACKNOWLEDGEMENTS

THE work of compiling material for a book involves many people, and I would like to take this opportunity to thank those organisations and private individuals who have given their assistance.

In particular I would like to thank the following organisations for the provision of information and photographs: The Science Museum, London; The American Library, at London University; the National Maritime Museum; P & A Campbell Ltd.; Red Funnel Steamers; David McBrayne Ltd. I am especially grateful to the following individuals: Mr. Smeaton of G.S.N. for the loan of books and the gift of the picture of *Crested Eagle,* Mr. William Watkins of the London Tugowners Association for the loan of the book 'A Hundred Years of Towage', Mr. W. Brooks of Normandy Ferries, Mr. Colin Dixon of Bass Charrington Ltd., Captain Don Hickman of the *Princess Elizabeth,* Miss Muriel Wilson, St. Albans City Librarian, and Mr. Oliver Smith, Editor of Ships Monthly.

In addition I wish to pay tribute to those who have encouraged me by their interest and support. I would like to thank Mr. Frank Ferneyhough and Mr. Keith Ellis for their help and advice. I am indebted also to my colleague and fellow-writer, Mrs. Muriel Miller, who assisted me with my research and constructively criticised each chapter. Last, but not least, my thanks to my wife, who typed the final draft and tolerated many hours of candle-burning, and my son for his loyal support and interest.

BIBLIOGRAPHY

Armstrong, Warren—*Atlantic Highway*
Bowen, Frank—*A Hundred Years of Towage*
Burtt, F.—*Steamers of the Thames and Medway*
Cornford, L. Cope—*A Century of Sea Trading*
Coton, R. H.—*A Decline of the Paddle Steamer*
Duckworth, C. L. D. and Langmuir, G. E.—*West Coast Steamers, Clyde River and other Steamers*
Gibbs, Commander C. R. Vernon—*British Passenger Liners of the Five Oceans*
Hancock, H.—*Semper Fidelis*
Lane, C. D.—*American Paddle Steamboats*
Mudie, Ian—*Riverboats*
Parsons, R. H. and Tolley, J. C.—*Paddle Steamers of Australasia*
Patterson, A. J. S.—*The Golden Years of the Clyde Steamers*
Rolt, L. T. C.—*Isambard Kingdom Brunel*
Spratt, H. Philip—*Birth of the Steamboat*
Stromier, George—*Steamers of the Clyde*
Thornley, F. C.—*Steamers of North Wales*
Thornton, E. C. B.—*South Coast Pleasure Steamers*
Thurston, Gavin—*The Great Thames Disaster*
Winchester, C.—*Shipping Wonders of the World*
Other sources of information were:
Ships Monthly, Sea Breezes, Paddle Wheels, and *Bristol Evening Post.*

INDEX OF PADDLE STEAMERS

INDEX OF PADDLE STEAMERS

INDEX OF PADDLE STEAMERS

INDEX OF PADDLE STEAMERS

GENERAL INDEX

Campbell, Robert, 96, 97, 123
Cannon, John, 166
Carttar, Charles Joseph, 62, 65
Channel Excursion Steamers Limited, 148
Channel Steamship Company, 70
Cinque Ports Steam Navigation Company, 148
Citizens Company, 42
City of Dublin Steam Packet Company, 25, 89, 108, 111
City of London Rifles, 113
Clacton Pier Company, 43
Claxton, Christopher, 34, 36, 37
Clydebank Shipbuilding & Engineering Company, 144
Clyde Shipping Company, 50, 157
Clyde Steamship Owners' Association, 97
Coastal Steam Packet Company, 190, 191
Cochrane, Thomas, Earl of Dundonald, 86
Collins, Edward, 29, 30, 31
Collins Line, 29, 31
Colwyn Bay & Liverpool Steam Packet Company, 114
Cortis, Anthony & Company, 16
Cosens & Company, 132, 140, 141, 142, 143, 144, 145, 146, 147, 148, 149, 150, 151, 152, 186
Cosens, Captain, 138, 139
Cunard Company, 21, 23, 27, 29
Cunard, Samuel, 23, 26, 27, 28, 30, 31

D'Abbans, Marquis de Jouffroy, 12
Dartmouth Steam Packet Company, 134
Deering, F. C., 148
Denny Brothers, 104, 195
Devon Dock, Pier & Steamship Company, 132, 133
Devon Steamship Company, 131
Dicey, Captain, 68
Ditchburn & Mare, 71
Dix, Christopher, 59, 63
Dorman Museum, 194
Duke, J. H. & J., 23
Dunkirk Veterans' Association, 188, 190
Dusting, W., 131, 132

Earle Company, 69
Eastern Counties Railway, 47
Eastern Railway Ferry, 48
Eastern Steam Navigation Company, 74, 76, 77
Eastham Ferry, 116

Eastham Ferry Pleasure Gardens & Hotel Company, 116
East India Company, 83
Eckford, Henry, 162
Edwards, Robertson & Company, 125, 127, 128
Ellet & Matthews, 131
Eltringham, J. T. & Company, 193
Ericsson, John, 177
Eyres, John, 59, 60, 63, 64, 65

Fairfield Shipbuilding & Engineering Company, 44, 104, 105, 111, 112, 120, 121, 185
Fairplay (screw tug), 190
Field, Joshua, 83, 89
Fitch, John, 13, 66, 90, 168
Forrester, G. & Company, 83
Fortes, Messrs. 188
Fox, 87
Firth of Clyde Steam Packet Company, 96
Fryer, Robert, 71
Fulton, Robert, 14, 15, 67, 161, 162, 163, 164
Furness Railway Company, 122

Galloway, Elijah, 89
Galway Line, 31
General Steam Navigation Company, 49, 50, 51, 52, 53, 124, 179, 185, 190
Gilbey's Gin, 191
Glasgow & Inverary Steamboat Company, 95
Glasgow, Paisley & Greenock Railway, 93
Glasgow & South Western Railway, 101, 102, 103, 104
Glasgow Steamers Limited, 101
Gourley Brothers, 55
Government of Bengal, 31
Graham, Sir James, 174
Great Britain (steamship), 21, 73, 74
Great Eastern Railway, 116
Great Eastern Steamship Company, 79
Great Ship Company, 77
Great Western Railway Company, 34, 134
Great Western Steamship Company, 24, 25, 31, 33, 34, 38, 39
Greenock & Wemyss Railway Bill, 93
Grey, William & Company, 192
Grinstead, Captain, 59, 60, 63, 64
Group 4 Committee (L.M.S./L.N.E.R.), 107

GENERAL INDEX

Gunn, John, 128, 140
Guppy, Thomas, 34, 36

Hall, Samuel, 87, 88
Hall, William John, 50
Halfpenny Fare Steamers, 88
Harrison, Captain (*Bywell Castle*), 64
Harrison, Captain (*Great Eastern*), 77
Hart, Alexander, 13
Hastings, St. Leonards & Eastbourne Steamboat Company, 139
Hedges, Kate, 125
Henderson, D. & W., 96
Hepple & Company Limited, 192
Hero of Alexandria, 11
Hickman, Don, 190
Hill, Charles & Son, 185
Horsley Iron Works, 18, 19
Horticultural College, 70
Hosken, Lieut. James, 37, 38
Heyghen, Van, Messrs., 189
Humber Ferry, 192
Hutchinson, David & Company, 94
Hutson & Corbett, Messrs., 126

Inglis, A. & J., 94, 104, 187, 192
Inverary Company, 100
Isle of Man & Liverpool Shipping Company, 119, 120
Isle of Man, Liverpool & Manchester Steamship Company, 120, 121
Isle of Man Steam Packet Company, 113, 118, 119, 178

Jack, Andy, 163
Jamieson, Jesse, 167
Joint Railways Fleet, 147, 148

King, Enoch, 167
Kibble, John, 71

Lady Ritchie, 56
La French, George, 116
Laird, John, 174
Lang, Oliver, 175
Lawrence, Theodore, 124
Leathers, Thomas, 166, 167
Leonardo da Vinci, 11
Leslies of Hebburn, 70
Liverpool & Douglas Steamers Limited, 121
Liverpool, Llandudno & Welsh Coast Steamship Company, 108, 111, 125
Liverpool & North Wales Steamship Company, 46, 111, 112, 113, 114

'Live Oak' George Law, 163
Livingston, Robert, 162, 163, 164
Lloyd George, David, 103
Loch Lomond Steamboat Company, 106
London, Brighton & South Coast Railway, 147
London, Chatham & Dover Railway Company, 70, 121
London County Council, 46, 47, 107
London, Midlands & Scottish Railway, 104, 105, 107
London, North Eastern Railway, 104, 105, 107, 186
London & South West Railway Company, 121, 147
London Steamboat Company, 58, 61, 64
London, Woolwich & Clacton-on-Sea Steamship Company, 43
Long, George (*Bywell Castle*), 64
Lord Dundas of Kerse, 13, 14

McBrayne, David, 94, 95, 100
McIver, David, 27
McKnight, S. & Company, 127, 141
McPhail, Captain, 102
Manby, Aaron, 18, 19
Manby, Charles, 18, 19
Margate Steam Packet Company, 53
Maudslay, Henry, 72
Maudslay, Joseph, 83, 84
Maudslay, Sons & Field, 23, 35
Maze, Peter, 34
Medway Queen Trust, 188
Medway Queen Yacht Marina, 189
Medway Steam Packet Company, 46
Melville, Lord, 174
Mersey Trading Company, 114
Miller, Patrick, 12, 13, 19
Millport Town Council, 103
Monks Ferry, 116
Morecambe Steamboat Company, 122
Murdoch, 84
Murray Valley Coaches Limited, 172

Napier, Admiral Sir Charles, 18, 19
Napier, David, 83, 87
Napier, David (Loch Lomond), 106
Napier, Robert, 25, 27, 28, 54, 81, 106, 118, 119

206